Armagnac

Armagnac

The Spirit of Gascony

C. E. Page

BLOOMSBURY

© Antler Books Ltd
First published in 1989 by
Bloomsbury Publishing Ltd.
2 Soho Square,
London W1V 5DE

ISBN 0-7475-0263-3

Produced by John Stidolph
Edited by Peter Fitzmaurice
Designed by Peter Hedges
Maps by Jeremy Dixon

Colour separations by Fotographics Ltd
Typesetting and mono origination by
Ace Filmsetting Ltd
Printed by BPCC Paulton Books Ltd

Contents

Acknowledgments

No book of this kind can be compiled without a great deal of local help. First I am grateful to all the many small proprietors who welcomed me – even when they said: "for heaven's sake, no publicity!" Next, to Monsieur Jean-Louis Martin, Director of the *Bureau National Interprofessionnel de l'Armagnac*, for the supply of essential statistics and names/addresses I might otherwise not have found. Madame Odile Bordaz, Director of the *Musée du Gers* in Auch, kindly furnished me with a most informative offprint concerning the Marquis de Bonas; Monsieur Pierre-Yves Péchoux of the *Université de Toulouse Le Mirail* has been tireless in supplying both learned treatises and putting me in touch with other persons who have specialised knowledge of the subject and who have been equally generous in answering my questions.

I owe a special debt to John Thorne of Dagenham, dealer in books concerning wines and spirits, who supplied me with copies of rare material I could not afford to buy. And I owe the early nineteenth-century American newspaper advertisements to the keen eye of Albert Shaw in David Godfrey's newspaper emporium in Kinnerton Street, London.

My files are thick with letters from so many helpful people that it would add another chapter if I were to mention them all, but I mention Marjorie McNinch and Diane Partnoy of the Hagley Museum and Library, Wilmington, Delaware, to demonstrate the geographical extent of the assistance I have received during my researches.

The illustrations have come from many sources, but I should like to single out Michael Walker at Food and Wine from France, Beth Connock of Air France, Jean Terrieux of *Maison de la France* and David Plunkett of Matthew Clark and Sons for their help.

John Stidolph and David Reynolds believed in this book. Their support, encouragement and patience has seen me through some bad luck and ill health. I reserve my final thanks for my friend Michael Hodson for his generous hospitality in the region and for all the running around and telephoning on my behalf.

C. E. Page
June 1989

Preamble

Happy the man, whose wish and care
A few paternal acres bound,
Content to breathe his native air,
In his own ground.

*T*hese lines from Pope's 'Ode on Solitude' seem apt to introduce Gascony and the Gascons. And the word Preamble is certainly more suitable than the word Preface, since we shall be looking, among other things, at the *alembics ambulants* of the Armagnac region. These portable stills amble from farm to farm looking not unlike ancient steam-rollers – a reminder of more leisurely days.

You would do well, if you follow this guide, to follow their example: to amble rather than rush through the Gascon countryside. For it is all too easy to miss weatherbeaten signs reading *produits régionaux / floc / armagnac* at the entrance of some small homestead, or unsignposted lanes leading to such, unless you adopt the motto 'go slow' and pay heed to my maps very closely.

There are other reasons for going slow. Hidden *châteaux* and solitary churches abound in this secret country. The *châteaux* are not grand, like those of the Loire, and few of them are open to the public: they remain private homes. Some do not announce their presence, or the fact that they, too, produce armagnac. Perhaps they were better called manor-houses than *châteaux*. If you stop to admire a local church, you may well find it closed, with a small card pinned to the door telling you where the key is to be had. This could be at the nearest *mairie* – but will you find the mayor in, or out in the fields tending his vines . . .? Let patience be your watchword. Sit in the nearest café and sip a small glass of armagnac. It has probably been produced by the mayor or a neighbour of his, or the café-

Left: Promising sign to Domaine Lesquette, near Manciet.
Right: Château de Salles, Salles d'Armagnac.

owner's brother-in-law – who knows? Why not ask, should you happen to like it?

There are many discoveries still to be made, apart from those listed and mapped here. Of the 15,000 or so wine-growing farmers in the region, some 1,400 distil their own produce. Others may have it distilled by professional *bouilleurs de cru*, yet sell it under their own label. Others again sell all their crop to a *cave co-opérative*, where some very good armagnacs are made and bottled – vintages even. The excellence of the co-ops is shown by the fact that they often win prizes at blind tastings. So do not be put off by their looking a bit like oil refineries: let your nose and palate be the judge. You will find a list of recent prize-winners at the end of this book. If some of the names best known in England are not among them, that is hardly my fault – simply all the more reason for this book.

The same applies to many of the places to stay which I mention. Again, only very few are listed elsewhere. Maybe they are too basic for our old friend *Bibendum* . . . I just do not know. Even that useful standby, the *Guide de Logis et Auberges de France* ignores all but a small handful. Indeed, the Gers *département* has no local affiliation chamber for *Logis*.

Which brings me to the Gascons, a race apart, fiercely individualistic. It is almost impossible to get them to join associations of any kind. They must be the despair of all the advertising fraternity: not only do they believe firmly that good wine needs no bush, they positively hide their light under a bushel. Promotion happens almost by default, and the annual fair and *'concours'* at Eauze remains more important than national or international ones.

Of course there are people that would have it otherwise. But the fact remains that around 40% of armagnac never leaves the region and of the rest, another 80% is sold within France, mainly to great restaurants and private buyers in Paris. Despite all the efforts of some of the larger, cognac-affiliated *négociants* – blenders of that 'cognarm' I shall be investigating later – your died-in-the-wool Gascon would rather retain his best armagnacs for himself. And the colour of your money or a blank cheque will make no difference if he does not like the cut of your jib. Even if he does, you will be rationed: I have just heard of a consignment of seven cases (i.e. 84 bottles) of a great old armagnac shipped by the owner of a *domaine* to his UK importer who happens to be a close personal friend. No wonder you can pay up to 150 francs per *degustation* in leading

L'Armagnac
Marcel TRÉPOUT
En Gascogne

Monastère Notre-Dame

VIC-FEZENSAC (GERS) Tél. 62.06.33.83

The Monastry of Notre Dame has been owned by the family of Marcel Trépout since 1926. The armagnac goes back to 1893!

Paris restaurants. (And the cheapest, in one restaurant I know of, is 35 francs per measure.)

But this compares, or contrasts if you like, with some quite acceptable younger armagnacs, to be bought at source for no more than 70–80 francs per 70cl bottle. When I say younger I mean seven or eight years old rather than twenty or more. This is cheaper than most eight-year-old malt whiskies and the comparison holds as you get to twenty or twenty-one-year-olds. The point being, of course, that you buy your whiskies through a chain of two or three middlemen, all of whom want their cut – not forgetting such overheads as extensive and ever more expensive promotion, as the whisky barons chase what is known as market share. Your small armagnac farmer could not care less about this: he will be quite happy to sell half of what he makes and put by the rest for a rainy day, or for his daughter's dowry in years to come. In fact, if he sold more than half of what he made, how would he accumulate the stocks necessary for older and better blends? Or ever get to the stage of offering a 'vintage reserve'?

The pros and cons of this question, and the way it is settled, will determine the future of armagnac. Much as I would like to see more armagnac, and a greater variety of armagnacs, on sale in the UK, I half hope that the sturdy independence of native Gascons will prevent any over-rapid expansion. Recently, too, the USA has made formidable forays into the region and is now Armagnac's biggest export market; and I have visions (or nightmares) of what happened to Burgundy prices some years ago when the Americans suddenly took a fancy to that region.

17

Gimet, one of the top names in distilling, also matures and blends his own armagnac.

As we shall see as we amble along, armagnacs to be sold by way of normal trade routes, and mainly in the three-star or VSOP class, are a very different product from what is – or should be – our main concern. And anything better needs to be produced at a snail's pace rather than ambling. There are no short cuts. In that sense, raiders of the 'yuppie' kind are best kept at bay, or we may not be drinking the finer types of armagnac in the twenty-first century. Fortunately, your true Gascon seems to care little for takeovers or expansion, but is content to live by Pope's maxim.

There are at least half-a-dozen factors that affect the nature and quality of any armagnac –

(1) the soil
(2) the grape varieties used
(3) the weather in any given year
(4) the manner of harvesting
(5) the manner of distilling and the skill of the distiller
(6) the manner of maturing

Of these, (3) above is perhaps the least important, for armagnacs may be blended from several different years. As indeed also of different grape varieties. We therefore get a seventh possible factor: the skill of the blender. And an eighth could be the skill of the cellar-master in deciding just when such blending is to take place and/or when to transfer the spirit from new, and generally small, oak casks to larger and older ones.

This last is debatable and in fact being debated all the time. There are those who maintain that the raw spirit should be left undisturbed all the time. After all, does it not, as it ages, age the casks too? Other producers do not care for new casks at all, especially if imported from outside the region. A much larger cask, already well used, is preferred, and of the local dark oak at that. The larger the cask, the slower the ageing process – and also, be it added, the smaller the loss by way of evaporation ('the angels' share', as it is known by all distillers).

Conversely, there are those who fuss over their newly and not-so-newly distilled armagnacs as if they were delicate children or fragile plants. Even when they do not change the contents from one kind of cask to another, they will change the positions of casks within the *chai* frequently: first under the roof, fairly dry and warm, later on the ground, fairly cool and humid.

You will find as many different opinions on such matters as there are 'experts'. I put the word, advisedly, into inverted commas; for every armagnac producer will, of course, defend his own methods vigorously. Truth in such matters is relative; what matters ultimately is whether the final result pleases you or me or enough other customers.

Are there, then, no absolute standards? The purist will maintain that there are. All armagnacs must be distilled in the *alembic armagnacais*, by means of a single, continuous process, to issue from this distillation at between 52 to 58 degrees alcohol. It must then be allowed to mature in local oak only (nothing imported from the more northerly Limousin or Tronçais forests, as used in the Cognac region), preferably grown on the owner's estate and with the making of casks supervised if not actually carried out by himself. The vines, of course, must also be of his own provenance, not bought from some other grower or distilled by anyone but himself. And reduction of the distilled product by means of demineralised water or even *petites eaux* to what is deemed the desired proof strength before bottling is taboo: the ageing process itself should be sufficient over the years (probably nearer twenty than ten) to soften the spirit.

Which explains, of course, why there are so few really fine armagnacs around, and why these are prohibitive in cost. For if the armagnac has taken twenty years to mature, the oak-tree has taken 100, and the seasoning of the wood before it is turned into staves for casks may well take another fifteen. The vines, of course, may yield their fruit from seven to eight-years old – and plentifully too. But 40-year-old vines yield many fewer grapes, albeit of much higher quality. All of which

19

The ambulant alembic armagnacais.

conspires to make a truly great armagnac very much of a waiting game.

Of course, you can get an acceptable eight-year-old armagnac, just as you can get an acceptable eight-year-old cognac or malt whisky. But it cannot be the same as a twenty-year-old. There are no short cuts. If you lay down an armagnac (in cask, I mean) for your godson this year, let him drink it when he is allowed to, maybe in eighteen years' time. (Though that might be a bit of a waste, given the tastes of the young 'upwardly mobile': an 81-year-old might appreciate it more!)

An air of tradition hovers around the Janneau premises in Condom.

Introduction

*T*his book will, I hope, be provocative enough to annoy quite a number of people – especially within the trade. As trades go, the wines and spirits trade is no worse than most and better than some. Still, in any trade the profit motive rules first and foremost; and if you are primarily interested in profits you should not be dealing with armagnac.

Armagnac, as I have found, is a vocation, not a profit-making venture. It is grown (or the best of it, anyway) as part of a mixed agricultural economy in which wine and cereals are predominant. Wines, as grown in that small south-western corner of France known as Gascony, mature rapidly and are palatable though not great. Within a year or so the wine farmer will have sold his produce at a profit. Maize is even more profitable, in that it is needed for force-feeding those millions of geese needed to produce *foie gras*, a luxury much esteemed both locally and abroad. (The French government actually pays a *prime* of 10,000 francs per hectare to farmers who uproot their vines and plant maize instead.)

Consider now the case (or better a cask?) of armagnac. The local oak from which the cask is made will be around 100 years old. When that oak has been felled, it needs to be seasoned for at least another ten years (some say nearer 20). The wine from which armagnac is made yields just one litre of spirit from ten litres of wine. It then has to remain in cask for at least ten years, maybe again nearer twenty, to yield a fine armagnac . . . At which point I hear cries of 'rubbish!' and the controversy begins. The men from Cognac who have invaded the region are up in arms. They have brought in their double stills and their Limousin or Tronçais oak and will produce you a passable VSOP in five years or so.

This 'cognarm', as I like to call it (recalling with some irony that in my native German *arm* means 'poor'), is good enough

Two grape presses from the Musée de L'Armagnac; the one above dates from the 18th century.

to fool the quaffers of Beaujolais Nouveau and suchlike. The harsh nature of the young, raw product is masked by a judicious addition of caramel and *le boisé*. Finally, of course, the spirit is reduced to the standard 40° (Gay-Lussac scale) alcohol. A nice touch, this: you make things easier for HM Excise while at the same time the addition of water dilutes the expensive spirit. I assure you, without fear of contradiction this time, that 95% of the stuff on sale in England is thus doctored (and you may read that last word, if you like, in the sense of 'emasculated').

Let us now return to Gascony, beginning this time at the end. No true armagnac-lover will sanction any dilution of the spirit. He will maintain that it should be bottled at 'barrel-proof' as and when it has reached its full maturity and optimum quality. Such ageing (I mean the length of it) will depend on a number of factors: e.g. has it remained in new casks throughout its life, or been transferred to other ones, the latter perhaps much larger as well as older, having lost much

Chateau de Pomès Pébérère

PRUNEAUX D'AGEN A L'ARMAGNAC

18% Alc.Vol.   50cl

Armagnac 22,50 cl à 40% vol., pur sucre, pruneaux. Poids net 500 g environ.

Louis Faget
Condom Gers France

Propriétaire récoltant   Marque déposée

of their tannin? Every small producer, who is usually also his own cellar-master, has his own particular methods. Hence the variety of good armagnacs that are to be found <u>in the region.</u> And hence this book, to guide you to them. The producers are one and all passionate about the quality of their armagnacs – remember that word 'vocation' in my second paragraph above?

Hence also certain omissions even among the best grower/ producers. There is no point in guiding you to properties where the owners will say to you politely but firmly 'sorry – I have none for sale'. For be assured of three things:

(1) some of the best armagnacs are <u>never</u> for sale: they remain within the family for generations, as treasured heirlooms, perhaps to be passed on by way of dowry when there is a daughter rather than a son to be considered;

(2) some proprietors sell only to the restaurant trade, often *en primeur* (a phrase which is probably known to you via your wine merchant) – i.e. very young – leaving it to the buyer to mature in cask and finally bottle, thus saving on heavy financing over the years;

(3) some just do not have enough for the casual passer-by or tourist: all they can afford to sell goes to regular customers by mail order, either within the region or throughout France – very little abroad, once again.

Note, please, that phrase 'all they can afford to sell'. The truly dedicated producer will be more concerned to preserve his stocks than to increase his turnover and/or profits.

So now, good hunting! And if you have little time to hunt, I can do no better than refer you at once to p. 152. If you have time to spare, I suggest you simply get lost among the many little lanes, often unsignposted, that lead off minor roads. A true farm armagnac sampled in a farm kitchen can be a pleasant surprise – and what better than making your own discoveries?

The rugged independence of the Gascon.

The 14th-century cloister and tower at La Romieu.

The Spirit of Gascony

I ought, I suppose, to begin by explaining or at any rate elucidating, the sub-title of this book. Armagnac and Gascony are not synonymous. Although armagnac (the alcoholic spirit) is produced entirely within the rather vague limits of what we loosely call Gascony today, by no means all of Gascony produces it. And both Gascony and Armagnac have known strictly defined borders in their day. The *comté* or earldom of Armagnac had its often-changing boundaries in medieval days, as did Gascony, which ended up as a province of France in 1598, under King Henry IV. This province then continued unchanged until France was divided into *départements* at the time of the French Revolution. Of this province, Armagnac was one of the administrative sub-divisions, as were the Lomagne, the Condomais, the Chalosse and others. And that administrative area is by no means the same as that which, around the middle of the nineteenth century, became known (for vinous purposes) as the Armagnac region, with its divisions into Haut, Bas and (wedged between them) the Ténarèze.

The known history of Gascony stretches back into pre-Roman times. But perhaps we should first define Gascony, which at one time stretched from the Pyrenees up north to Bordeaux and even beyond. For our purposes, we had best look at it as the region south of the river Garonne. I would set its north-western limits at Marmande (which falls just inside the present *département* of Lot-et-Garonne), then follow the curve of the river south-east to Toulouse, where it turns south-west towards Saint-Gaudens. If we then follow the N117 through Tarbes and Pau to Bayonne on the Atlantic coast, we shall have done no more than skirt the Pyreneean foothills and the Basque country. All of this was at one time part of the kingdom of Béarn and Navarre, and deemed to be part of

Gascony. So too was the north-west, even though we are here touching on what is known as the Bordelais.

Village in the Gers.

If you look at a map which shows France divided into *départements*, you will see that we have touched upon eight different ones, counting the Gironde which we need to pass through, via Bazas and Labouheyre, to complete our very rough circle to Bayonne. You will also see that one *département* lies at the heart of it all: the Gers.

And so it would be right and proper to call the Gers the heart of Gascony. It is also the heart of Armagnac, though small bits of the *appellation controlée* fall within the Landes and Lot-et-Garonne *départements*. And it is with the Gers (which they decided to call Armagnac when they first divided France from provinces into *départements* in 1790, only to change their minds later to call it by the river which more or less bisects it from south to north) that I shall mainly deal.

It is quite big enough; you could easily question the inclusion of Toulouse as belonging more to the Languedoc than to Gascony. But Toulouse comes into our story, because distilling most probably reached Armagnac via this city, just as Bayonne and Bordeaux come into it because armagnac (the spirit) passed through these ports.

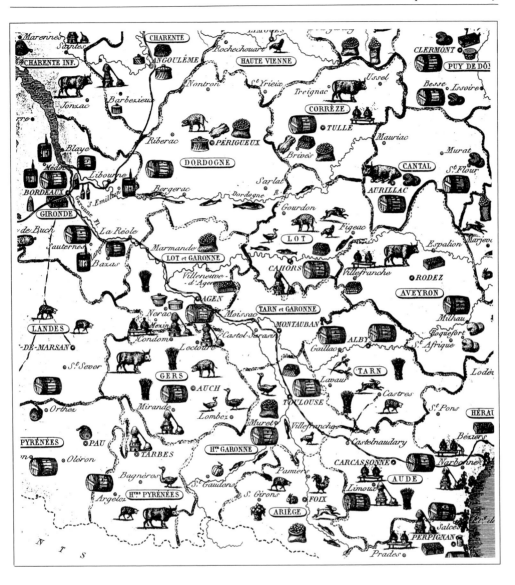

A gastronomic map of France, dated 1861,

Look at the map again and draw another line: this time from Nérac to Pau. You will see that there are, in fact, alternative routes. But if you take the one passing through Mézin, Eauze and Nogaro, you will be passing through some of the best Armagnac country. At Riscle, where you cross the river Adour, you are within a very few miles of Maumusson-Laguian and already in A.O.C. Madiran red wine region. You are also on the old pilgrim trail to St Jacques de Compostelle, or one of them, anyway. And you will pass further south, on your way to Pau, through Lembeye and Morlaas, of which more anon.

31

The Gers is, even today, the most intensely agricultural *département* of France, with a larger population than elsewhere gaining a living from the land. By which I mean geese, ducks and cereals as much as wines and spirits.

Prière du Gascon. It doesn't scan, but it makes sense.

Today, of course, this has its advantages, for those who dislike fuming factory chimneys or railway lines disfiguring the landscape. The roads of Gascony are as good as any in France, with a blessed absence of *autoroutes* and concomitant outcrops of motorway cafés, motels and other such horrors. Instead, pleasant wayside inns a-plenty and *fermes-auberges* tucked away in the rolling countryside. Once more, Gascon pride brings with it both its rewards and its penalties. You will look almost in vain for anything listed in either *Michelin* or the *Guide des Logis de France*. I think there are five establishments in all listed in the latter's 1988 edition for the Gers, and there is no local affiliated chamber, as in most other *départements*. Do not let this put you off, however: you will find food and lodging as good as elsewhere, and at prices unbelievably reasonable, if you follow my recommendations or those of Monsieur Vidal's *Guide de Gascogne*.

But I anticipate. Let us look a little more closely at the spirit of Gascony in the figurative sense. Everyone who knows a little about the Gascons knows that they are fiercely individualistic, fiery and impetuous, brave and generous to a fault. In fiction, these qualities have been immortalised by the figures of d'Artagnan (the fourth musketeer of Dumas' stories), and by Cyrano de Bergerac in Rostand's play. But these had true models, many of whose traits remain true today. What mixture of influences was it which brought this about?

We do not know much about the original Gascons. They were certainly of part-Spanish stock, part-Basque (hence perhaps the Roman name Vasconia). We do know that from Roman times onwards there was a constant stream of invasions. After the Romans came the Visigoths, who established a huge kingdom, stretching from the Loire to southern Spain, with their capital at Toulouse. Then came the Franks, who finally defeated the Moors (the latter, of course, having conquered Spain and having designs across the Pyrenees too). Each successive wave of invaders brought new blood into the region. The Spanish influence remains to this day in bullfights during the summer months; Estang and Eauze are among the towns which have *arènes* for this purpose.

And then came the English, laying claim to the region on tenuous links with Eleanor of Aquitaine. Why not push further south from Bordeaux, indeed? The Hundred Years' War, and more especially the Black Prince, brought much devastation.

D'Artagnan pops up everywhere!

But they also brought a new kind of medieval architecture: the fortified towns or villages built round a central square, known as *bastides*. Many of them survive today, despite more wars and civil disturbances. One of them, actually known as Labastide d'Armagnac, is today one of the principal distilling centres for that other spirit of Gascony.

That other spirit arrived just around the time when the English were finally driven out (today's invasion being very modest and quite different in character, as we shall see later). We shall, in a subsequent chapter, follow it through the centuries, watch its progress and occasional reverses, assess its position in the international spirits market today and, finally, try and look a little into the future.

Here it will be enough to stress its difference from that other great brandy, cognac, and to proclaim loudly and firmly *Vive la difference*! The best armagnac is, like the best cognac, inimitable, and reflects profoundly the fiery, complex spirit of those who make it with such love and care.

Their complexity is part of their charm; ultimate finesse not necessarily so. The fact that there are almost as many different opinions as to what constitutes a fine old armagnac as there are producers only adds to the joy of the chase. I hope this guide leads you to at least some of whom you approve and to make more discoveries of your own.

The Secret Spirit

Although there can be no doubt that armagnac was distilled a century or even two before cognac, it remained for a long time practically unknown except locally. Just how little known (despite claims by the Gascons on the contrary) is shown by the fact that there is no mention of the word *armagnac* (as a noun denoting the spirit, not the region with capital 'A') in the great *Littré*, 1956 edition. And when the even bigger and better *Robert* dictionary in 20 volumes at long last gives an entry for it, the first illustration of its use is dated 1846 – which must have been arrived at after considerable research. Previous to this, apparently, it had always been preceded by the words *eau de vie (d'Armagnac)*. Cognac, by contrast, had passed into the language early in the seventeenth century, and imports of it to England are known from 1687 onwards, as proved by an advertisement in the *London Gazette* of that year.

Who first shipped armagnac to England, and when, remains obscure. Dufor cites an English *négociant*, Henry Thompson of Bordeaux, buying 10,800 *livres*-worth of *eau de vie* during 1647/8. But as he shipped it to Middelburg in the Netherlands and the nature of the spirit is not specified, it may have been brandy of some other region. (Incidentally Thompson's name is the only English one to appear in Dufor's almost 300 pages, and we shall have more to say about that later.) We know, for instance, that the house of Augier in Cognac, which still exists, had been founded in 1643. We know also that grape brandies were being distilled not only in what are now the Charentes and Gers, but down to the Pyrenees and inland to the Tarn region: in fact, Dufor specifically mentions an *eau de vie de Gaillac* shipped in 1521. This appears to be the first time the actual source was named, i.e. long before Cognac even.

It is only fair to add that Dufor also mentions a *négociant* (or family firm) called Laborde-Lagrauley as known from 1643, at

Cazaubon – i.e. the same date as Augier at Cognac. But what Laborde-Lagrauley did remains a blank.

The town of Montreal in the Ténarèze.

How good (or how bad) armagnacs sold during the seventeenth century were we shall probably never know. We do know that right up to the early twentieth century, when in 1909 strictly delimited regions came into force, *frelatage* (adulteration or mixing with other grape brandies, including cognac) was not uncommon.

I am not saying that this was universal, simply that there was no law to prevent it before then, nor any control as to what happened to armagnac once it travelled outside the region in cask. And it is not until 1920, in Saintsbury's famous *Notes on a Cellar-Book* that we can trace (according to the great Oxford dictionary) some appreciation in English as to armagnac's particular qualities. It may be worth noting that the 1933 edition of the OED, like *Littré* of 1956, does not give armagnac at all: we find it only in the 1972 supplement.

Trade within France, of course, was somewhat different. But internal toll-taxes would have hampered its distribution there, too, before the French Revolution. Exceptions were doubtless made for the King's table; and we know the Marquis d'Ivry had supplies sent to Paris around 1750. But elsewhere? We read of it, still preceded by the words *eau de vie* (so that people might

The good brig JA\...
fail in five days for *Martinique*. ...
Freight or Paſſage, apply as above.
October 23

The first reference I have found to armagnac in the USA. An ad in the Boston Centinel, 23 October 1805.

, 1805.
,s, from St.
., Hammond,
Ward, Salem ;
both to ſail ve-
Union, Roundy,
ero, Appleton.—
t, in co. with the
d brig Swift, Bul-
: ſhip Bonnetta a-
50, lon. 39. Saw
13, 20, lon. 63, 40.
ſch. Mercator, 35

ier to obſerve
coaſt, that on
he tacked
uſe, W. S.
iin half
d of

Jonathan Davis,

No. 2, *Long-Wharf*   *Has for Sale,*

FRENCH BRANDY, 20 pipes old Cognac, 180
do Armignac ; 40 puncheons Jamaica Rum ;
8 do Antigua do of an excellent quality ; 150
cafes Claret Wine ; 36 tierces white Wine Vin-
egar ; 20 boxes white Havana Sugar ; a few tierces
Honey ; Ruſſia and Ravens Duck of the firſt quality ; Ruſſia Boltrope ; warranted Anchors, of all
ſizes ; Bills of exchange on London and Amſter-
dam.

For Sale, Freight or Charter,

THE brig DECATUR, of 141
tons, ſingle decked, a remarkable
fine Veſſel, 12 months old, compleat-
ly fitted, now lying at *Packard and
Earn's Wharf.*   Oct 23

W. O. Staves and Naval Stores.

THE Cargo of ſloop *Union*, conſiſting of
15 m. W O Pipe ⎫ STAVES.
1 m. do Hhd ⎭
oft Turpentine, 24 do T

F,
Win,
nock'i
fine, ſiue
bbls. 300 ,
India Salt P,

Athe.

HAVE rec
Bales
Flannels ; crin
Baize ; plated
mou do ; mo

No 22,

NOW
laſt

not confuse it with a wine, no doubt) in the *Almanach des Gourmands* of 1806. But how much, or how little was then sold in Paris, let alone abroad, remains obscure. Nothing in England, for sure, because of the Napoleonic wars.

North America is another intriguing puzzle. We should recall not only that the Dutch merchant fleet in the seventeenth century was the largest in the world, outnumbering the British by about four to one; that Amsterdam was an *entrepot* for the wines and spirits they bought in France; but also that New York was known as Nieuw Amsterdam until the Dutch ceded it to England in 1664. But were there shipments direct from Bayonne to America, or even via the Dutch Antilles? Doubtless spirits were shipped, but whether of pure or adulterated armagnac remains uncertain.

As a summary, we may say that even today only about twelve million bottles of armagnac are sold world-wide: one-tenth of cognac sales and one-hundredth of Scotch sales. No wonder the better armagnacs are already in short supply, and that the better producers find it more profitable to sell direct to the hotel and restaurant trade in France, rather than bother with exports now. Yet in ten years, exports to the USA have increased ten-fold. What if armagnac were to become as popular there as Scotch? We in England would find ourselves in a classic 'Burgundy' situation, with not enough to meet the demand – at least for the best, and at prices within reason.

Le Vert Galant

Henry IV (he always signed himself with a 'y', never with an 'i') is known and loved throughout France as *'Le Vert Galant'*. Loved is not too strong a word for this monarch who in 1589 united the Kingdom of France, who fought more than 100 battles and 200 sieges, and whose prowess as a lover (the evergreen gallant) was equal to that as a soldier. He was perhaps the only good king that France ever had, good in the sense of caring more for his subjects than for himself, popular in the sense of 'Good Queen Bess' of England or 'Old Fritz' of Prussia, all part of their own particular patriotic folklore.

To disentangle fact from legend here is by no means easy, but I shall try. He was born at Pau, capital of the Kingdom of Navarre, in 1553, the son of Jeanne and Henri d'Albret, and spent the first eight years of his life there, roughing it barefoot in the Pyrenees. He then went to Nérac, on the northern borders of what is today armagnac country, there to be educated in a manner more in keeping with his status as a prince. Memorials of his youth can therefore be found at both Pau and Nérac; near the latter are still the *Moulins de Barbaste* and *Guyèze*, used by him as hunting lodges. At the age of sixteen he fought his first battle. The Massacre of Saint Bartholomew in Paris (1573) was one he narrowly escaped by turning (or pretending to turn) Catholic. He changed his faith, it must be admitted, again later, fighting as a good Huguenot during the Wars of Religion, and yet again when it came to consolidating his kingdom with the famous quip 'Paris is well worth a Mass'.

Legend takes over already with his baptism: some say his lips were moistened with some drops of armagnac, others maintain it was with Jurançon sweet wine, as grown near Pau. Whether or not the letter he later wrote to his mistress Gabrielle d'Estrées is genuine or not, it certainly expresses his

joie de vivre: 'let us enjoy, my sweetest, this elixir of long life; the House of France can only gain by it in gallantry and valour; as God lives, dearest, nothing is comparable to armagnac.'

The Cathedral at Condom.

What else? We know that he encouraged agriculture, and especially viticulture throughout his kingdom. As a *bon viveur*, he appreciated wines from as far afield as the Jura, Burgundy and the Loire. But no more direct link with armagnac can be traced. It is, of course, possible that he took its distillation and consumption for granted; that, later on, the Bishop of Condom sent him regular supplies of it to Paris. The monks were, of course, the principal distillers at that time; the Condomais is again not far from Nérac; it was and is a principal distilling region. And it was at Nérac, at the court of 'good Queen Margot' (Henry's divorced first wife, said to be as dissolute as he himself in sexual matters), that the poet Salluste du Bartas wrote a long and exceedingly boring didactic poem called *La Septmaine* (on the seven days of the creation of the world, in which occurs quite incidentally, by way of comparison with some heavenly miracle, a passage describing the mysterious transmutation of wine to spirit which happens in the marvellous *alambic*: vapours rising to a head and dropping

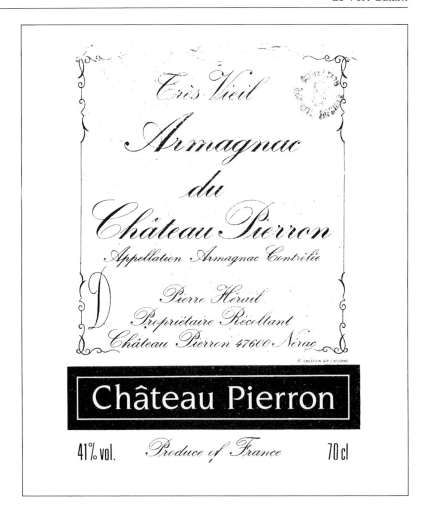

crystal-clear, drop by drop, into a glass below, with the subtlest of aromas).

We may be fairly sure that Henry IV would have known Salluste du Bartas; and that, if he did not appreciate the poem, he certainly appreciated the results as sketched here! The process described is of course not that of today, nor even that of the cognac still, but a much more primitive one involving glass vessels as used right up to the mid-seventeenth century, derived from Islamic medieval models.

I wish I could say more, and something more precise, about Henry IV's involvement with armagnac; but I must leave it with this rather circumstantial evidence. Only finally to lament that this merry and thoroughly humane ruler was to be killed by a half-crazed assassin in 1610 rather than die in his sleep with a bottle at his bedside.

A vintage picture of Larressingle, 13th-century fortified village.

English links with Gascony

A long love-hate relationship links England with France. Without going back to '1066 And All That', and the painful fact that half of us are probably half Norman rather than Anglo-Saxon today, a much stronger link was forged when Henry Plantaganet married Eleanor of Aquitaine, and we found ourselves with lands stretching from the Loire to the Pyrenees.

Temporarily, anyway; the claim to these possessions by marriage was soon contested. It needed the Hundred Years' War to settle it finally in favour of the French. What concerns us here is how it affected Gascony and (at least indirectly) armagnac.

The evidence is partly documentary, partly numismatic and partly architectural. Thus documents from the fourteenth century, still in the archives of Mézin, show that this town (today a centre of armagnac production) supplied wine to the King of England early during the century, before the Bordeaux monopoly was established. We know also of a number of *bastides* established by the English rather than the French at this time or even earlier: Montréal-du Gers, for instance, dates from 1289. This, like Mézin, is in the north of the region; further to the south the French built similar fortified towns and villages to repel further English advances – e.g. Mirande, very close to the borders of today's Pyrenean *départements*.

What are known as Anglo-Gallic coins were struck as far south as Bayonne during the days of the Black Prince, towards the middle of the fourteenth century. But English tenure of Gascon lands was always sporadic, rather than semi-permanent as further north, say from Bordeaux to Bergerac. All the English did with their frequent forays into the region was to lay waste the vineyards, villages, pillage the

43

countryside and generally strike terror into such of the inhabitants as were not murdered.

Even in traditional Gascony you would be hard pushed to find oxen in the fields today.

The biggest of such raids into Gascony, headed by the Black Prince himself, took place in 1355. The Count of Armagnac was an ally of the French King and thus disputing English sovereignty over what was then part of the Duchy of Aquitaine. Having once got the taste for looting, the Black Prince and his marauding horsemen carried the undeclared war much further south into Languedoc almost as far as the Mediterranean coast at Narbonne, a town at that time described as 'but little smaller than London'. It, like Carcassone, well fortified and defended, he failed to sack; likewise Toulouse. For the rest, and particularly within the boundaries of Armagnac, he wrought havoc; as one of his companion knights reported in a letter home: 'you may know for certain that the French King has never received such loss and destruction as in this raid' goes on to talk about the districts and fine towns that have been laid waste (including Nogaro and Plaisance in the heart of Armagnac). The Prince spared Bassoues, the property of the Archbishop of Auch, but burnt and sacked Samatan ('as great a town as Norwich') on the river Save; in a letter to the Bishop of Winchester he boasted of having ridden 'right across the land of Armagnac,

Manor house in Gers. Is maize displacing the vines? I fear so.

harrying and wasting the country, whereby the lieges of our most honoured lord the King, whom the count had formerly oppressed, were much comforted'. To which one can only comment 'some comfort . . .!' If not pillaged by one party, the Gascons were pillaged by another. (When the English were finally driven out in 1453, internecine strife continued among various factions, and the country knew no real peace until the end of the Wars of Religion between Protestants and Catholics with the accession of Henry IV).

Thus the second English invasion, coming over 450 years later, caused much trepidation and, in the event, a rather pleasant surprise. The Duke of Wellington, having conquered Spain, pursued the remnants of the Imperial army across south-west France from Bayonne to Toulouse. A merciless disciplinarian, he flogged or even hung any soldier trying to live off the country; every scrap of provisions, whether for man or beast, had to be paid for. The local populace welcomed him and his troops, therefore, almost as a liberator (Napoleon's own troops behaving very differently). At Bayonne, the Duke used the local mint for striking exact replicas of French gold coins (his army of ruffians containing a number of skilled forgers); soon, English soldiers were fraternising with French ones across the river Nive for brandy.

45

I had hoped, in this context, to come across the word armagnac; but it was not to be. Sir George Bell, whose *Rough Memoirs of an Old Soldier* give a fascinating account of all this, tells us of French soldiers shouting *'cognac'* across the river. What a let-down; but I believe him to be correct. No English soldier would have known the word 'armagnac' in 1814. But what about Sir George Bell himself, officer and gentleman? Quartered for some days in the very heart of the best Bas-Armagnac country, he speaks only of the excellent red wine offered to him and his fellow officers by their host at Aire-sur-Adour, and at his regret in failing to remember to take a magnum with him, as they had to depart in a hurry. No mention of spirits of any kind here – but should this really surprise us? Spirits were for the common soldier; a gentleman's post-prandial drink in those days was port or madeira; and I daresay the young George Bell still had some supplies of this with him from across the border.

We jump from 1814 to the 1970s now, when two enterprising Englishmen, Peter Hawkins and Christopher Oldham, decided on a totally peaceful invasion of Armagnac. The former, a civil engineer with interests in northern France, bought the *Domaine de Papolle* near Mauléon d'Armagnac; the latter, some years later, acquired the *Château de Lacaze* near Parlebosq. One being in the Gers *département*, the other in the Landes (but fairly close together all the same), they promptly set about colonising the natives by forming rival county cricket teams . . . Of their more serious efforts I cannot tell much. Christopher Oldham did not last very long; he turned the *Château de Lacaze* into a showpiece, ditto its cellars, wine and distilling equipment, sales offices with mini-skirted receptionists, computers *et al*, and then sold out to a Japanese conglomerate which I have no intention of advertising here. Whether to make a killing or cut his losses, I do not know. To my way of thinking, the Lacaze armagnacs are bottled far too young. Peter Hawkins has lasted rather longer, but how much longer is at the moment an unanswered question; he still spends much of his time in northern France. Whether absentee landlordism works for him or not I cannot say. I suspect that the locals have watched both these experiments with some amusement, though it is only fair to add that the *Domaine de Papolle* has won some gold medals for its products since Mr Hawkins took the estate over. Certainly, they are more to my taste than the Lacaze.

Controversy

*I*s there any other subject under the sun about which there are so many different opinions as about armagnac? And about which the holders of such opinions tend to be so opinionated? Controversies rage about old and new methods of distilling, for instance, about how best to mature the young spirit, about which is the best spirit, even about the bottles in which to sell it. I read in Christie's Wine Publication *Armagnac*, by the brothers Jean and Georges Samalens, that all self-respecting armagnac is sold in the *basquaise* of 70cl or 150cl, or in the *pot gascon* 250cl. 'Nonsense', said Monsieur Pierre Laberdolive to me on a recent visit to him, 'we always use the tall, upright *bordelaise*, or *cognacaise*, to hold 70cl.' (I myself prefer the term *bordelaise*, even if that holds 75 rather than 70cl – just look at the odd shapes of some cognac bottles!)

And what, when you come to look into it, is the traditional armagnac still? Prior to 1800, only the Charentais still was used in the Armagnac region. Admittedly, during the nineteenth century, the two were used as producers thought fit, and the 1800 still gradually took over, with many improvements culminating in that by Verdier (1899). Yet the use of the Charentais still was not prohibited in the Armagnac region until 1936, and it was re-introduced in 1972 . . .! A sole rule of 35 years or so can hardly be called, with any justification, time-honoured.

And thus we might, and indeed, shall go on, seeing many contradictions in the course of our exploration. Which is part of the charm of Armagnac the region, as of armagnac the spirit. As Cicero once wrote: 'consistency is the virtue of small minds', and the Gascons are anything but small-minded. Like Whitman, in their contradictions they contain multitudes.

Which makes, of course, for a multitude of armagnacs. True connoisseurs will tell you not only the *canton* from which each

'Farmagnac'. No doubt about it.

The cognac-type still. Progress or anathema?

came, but the very village. This has to do not only with methods of distilling, but with grape varieties used, the particular soil in which these were planted, and the oak of casks in which the spirit was matured. The oak of Le Frèche in the Landes, they will tell you, is different in character from that further east in the forest of Monlezun. And oak imported from the north, from the forests of Tronçais and Limousin, as used for cognac is at once recognizable, and highly controversial.

'*La basquaise*', continued Monsieur Laberdolive, as I continue now, '*c'est du commerce*'. Said somewhat loftily, as if commerce were a dirty word. And when you sell your bottles one by one, to crowned heads of Europe; when you have supplied the *Hotel de Paris* in Monte Carlo for three generations; when your 1904 vintage was offered to Kruschev at Pau in 1962 and you have people like Onassis, Fernandel and *Les Compagnons de la Chanson* beating a path to your farmyard door, you may well take a somewhat lofty view of humbler traders. He had just been in the process of packing and despatching a consignment of seven cases (all of 84 bottles) for his friend and agent Georges Barrière in London; I forgot to ask if this was a quarterly or half-yearly ration. You will not, as Monsieur Barrière kindly informed me, find it in

49

any shop; maybe in a dozen or so of the top London restaurants and a couple elsewhere in the country (no names, no packdrill, except to add that they are way beyond the pocket of a humble hack like myself).

Monsieur Laberdolive is among those happy owners who have century-old oak trees on their estates. He makes his own casks and distils his own wines, from three different *domaines*. He had, until they ceased to yield wine late in the 1940s, some pre-phylloxera *folle blanche* – old vines which had miraculously survived the pest. He allowed me to sample his 1935, recently bottled after more than 50 years in cask . . . words fail me as to its quality. No price was mentioned; he does not have anything so mundane as a printed tariff.

Why this digression? Because there are many grower/ producers like Monsieur Laberdolive, and many on a much more modest scale. They produce and bottle, say, between 1,500 to 5,000 bottles per year. And many of them will maintain that 50 years in cask does not necessarily give a 'wooden' taste to armagnac – or not to their particular armagnac, anyway. Yet you will find reference books that state fifteen years as ample and (maybe) 30 years as too long. Armagnac is said to mature more rapidly than cognac. Like most things that are said about armagnac this is only partly true.

Thus we read, for instance, that the Ténarèze is deemed less prized than the Bas-Armagnac, with the latter always referred to as the best region. I would myself say that it is a difference in kind, not in quality, though a cognac-trained palate might indeed prefer the smoother Bas, and others still swear by only the Grand-Bas, or armagnacs from the Landes rather than Gers *département*. Do such preferences really matter? Take Bordeaux by way of comparison; is a great Pomerol better than a great Médoc? Yet there are people who would mark them out of 100, as if they were schoolboys' essays.

Monsieur Hector Théaux is one of the grand old men of the Ténarèze, at Cazeneuve. He too sells a 1935 vintage; and this time there is a tariff: it will cost you 450 francs per 70cl bottle (or did, in May 1988, when I visited him). Please do not ask him for an export discount, or what it would be if you bought five cases. He is just not interested, his price is fixed and firm at 450 francs. A mass market does not entice him, let alone supermarkets; he sells to passers-by (not many from England, it seems) from all over Europe. He sells also, of course, to local

Barrel-making is a craft with room for no errors. The tolerances are very precise.

and Paris restaurants. And he will absolutely refuse to sell you more than 100 bottles or so.

So will Monsieur Dubourdieu of Lannes near Mézin. And this is where commerce begins to rear its ugly head, in the shape of the BNIA. Ten cases or more, and you must submit samples to this official body (watchdog) of the armagnac trade; there are forms to be filled in and dues to be paid. Who wants the bother? Certainly no proud Gascon who is sure of his product's quality and needs no official seal of approval. He will sell what he can, as and when he can – and what he does not sell may well be worth more in the years ahead.

I simplify of course; it is not as easy as that. There is capital outlay to be considered. A single cask costs over £150 now, and production costs per hectare have risen by over 50% during the past ten years. Taxes are prohibitive, it is not uncommon for them to account for 70% of turnover. *Négociants* with large stocks, as also the larger *co-opératives*, can cope more easily than the peasant farmer.

One recent concession has eased the position of such growers. When taxes were last increased in 1982, small producers with not more than 12 hectares and not distilling more than 50 hectolitres of alcohol, were exempted from this increase. This has led, happily, to a notable increase in the

number of such proprietors. Armagnacs bottled at source were prior to this concession something of a rarity, with a handful of large and old estates in the Bas accounting for over 75% of sales. During the past five years, there has been a marked shift, especially in the Ténarèze, which is beginning to come into its own after living for long in the shadow of the Bas.

This barrel is made from the wood of Limousin. More for cognac than for armagnac.

All I have been saying so far applies only to the top end of the market. The biggest sales are still in blends bottled by large *négoçiants*, or equally large *co-opératives*. And if export sales now account for 50% overall, it is less than 10% of this 50% that comes from the Bas or Ténarèze. In fact, I cannot recall seeing any Ténarèze, unblended and labelled as such on the shelves of London wine merchants known to me. SOPEXA (Food and Wine from France Ltd) is more concerned with advertising and boosting 'Armagnac – not the best known but known by the best', than such refinements as particular regions.

Yet the regions do matter, just as they <u>do</u> in Bordeaux for wines. Armagnac can never compete with cognac in volume terms; it can only compete on quality. Here, the similarity with malt whiskies is striking: they may only be a small fraction of what is sold by way of blends; they sell at a premium price after long ageing in cask: ten, twelve, fifteen years, even more. And the public has learnt to distinguish Islay malts from Speyside ones, to mention only the most common difference.

There are just a few signs that this is beginning to be understood, both here and in France. Meanwhile, the USA is forging ahead with sales that have now outstripped those in Japan. Not only the Eastern seaboard states now, but Texas and even Colorado are discovering the delights of smaller, estate-bottled producers, or their products, rather. When the Tilland Family Wine Co. of Denver can boast of importing a 1964 vintage from *Domaine de Maupas*, why can I not find it in England?

53

The Musée de l'Armagnac, at Condom.

Distillation in Gascony

No-one knows precisely when it all began. But we can guess how it all began, in the Middle Ages, through Moorish and other Islamic influences. Strange but true, distillation came to Europe via the Arabs, who at one time ruled not only Spain but also Sicily. We know, too, that their great medical school at Salerno in Sicily had close relations with the university of Montpellier in the Languedoc, not all that far from Toulouse. So we begin to hear of distilling practices in the region towards the end of the thirteenth century. I should emphasize here that all such distilling was for strictly medical purposes, and that herbs rather than wine served as a basis. (Islamic law concerning the consumption of alcohol would have been even more rigorously enforced then than it is now.)

Here then are a few key dates. The first western (as opposed to Arabic) writer on distillation was Arnaud de Villeneuve in 1285. He was, incidentally, doctor to the first French Pope – those Popes who were later to make Avignon their seat rather than Rome, and caused a great schism in the Catholic church for a century or so. But that is another story. More important, there is to be found in the archives at Moissac (Tarn-et-Garonne) a document dated 1348, which tells of a spirit still: an *alambic* used, in this instance, for the distillation of rose-hips. In 1411 we get the first indication as to the distilling of wine, this time in a document preserved in the Toulouse archives, by a certain Antoine; twenty years on, there is mention of a couple named Nouvel, apparently renowned for the quality of their *eau ardente* (fiery water).

All this, as also a famous manuscript found in Auch (the *Recettes Alchimiques*, giving some thirty different uses for distilled spirits), is still concerned with medical practice: a nip to cure the ague rather than send you reeling. Much more important, for our purposes is a document of 1431, from Vic-

CHATEAU DU
BUSCA-MANIBAN
NOBLE DEMEURE DU XVIIᵉ SIÈCLE DES MARQUIS DE MANIBAN

Armagnac

VISITE DU CHÂTEAU
DE PAQUES AU 15 OCTOBRE, TOUS LES JOURS (SAUF LE LUNDI) DE 14 à 18 H
PAR GROUPE SUR DEMANDE PAR TÉLÉPHONE
Tél. 62 29 12 02 - Tél. 62 28 34 52
D. 229 DE CASSAIGNE à LAGARDÈRE - 32310 MANSENCOME

The first recorded still in the Armagnac region was sited at Busca-Maniban in 1649.

Fezensac. This gives by way of inventory for inheritance purposes a list of the possessions of the local Count; among them, apart from distilling apparatus, are mentioned (a) a wine-press and (b) *tonneaux*, i.e. barrels or casks. Thus, for the first time, the latter are found in association with the distilling process.

Mind you, the links are still pretty tenuous. We do not know for certain when it was discovered that distilled spirits gained smoothness by being kept in cask: the Count may very well have used his casks for his wines rather than his spirits. We have a long way to go before we arrive at anything approaching the refinements of ageing brandies as practised today. What is perhaps most important is that now we are in the very heart of today's Armagnac country (look at the map, and you will see that Vic-Fezensac lies very near the centre of the present *appellation controlée*, in the Ténarèze just beyond the eastern boundary of Bas Armagnac). Before this, we have been moving around the periphery of the region, or even further afield. It is perhaps no accident that Vic-Fezensac remains, to this day, a centre of distillation, blending from the two best areas, and carries on a vigorous trade in armagnacs. More about all this in the appropriate pages.

I am not sure how much of this is relevant to our progress through subsequent centuries. It is highly relevant to Gascon pride in establishing their claim to be the first – long before the men of Cognac – to have distilled wines into spirits. They choose to forget, alas, that they remained in a kind of backwater, if not actual limbo, for at least another 200 years; that they were using what was to become the cognac-type still during all this time, and right into the first decades of the nineteenth century; that their spirit (possibly called armagnac since the late sixteenth century), albeit appreciated locally, served otherwise largely to fortify wines or the weaker cognacs.

Legend and fact are much intertwined during these centuries. It is said that Henry IV (*le Vert Galant*, as much a lover of wines as of women, and a true Gascon from the house of Albret) praised the qualities of armagnac in a letter to his mistress Gabrielle d'Estrées. There are doubts about the authenticity of this letter, as about the adventurous exploits of d'Artagnan: the real one, whose existence is not doubted, spent rather more time in dull, administrative duties at court than in fighting. Not for nothing has the word *gasconnade* passed into the French language as meaning vainglorious boasting (but never, unless you fancy a duel, remind a Gascon of this!).

This is perhaps the moment to take a quick look at the glassmakers of the region. Again, glass came to it from the Middle East (Islam) via Toulouse. The first *maître-verrier* we know of by name – and the glassmakers had their own craft guild – is one Jean de Granier, who made his appearance (again, in the region of Vic-Fezensac) during the early years of the eighteenth century. His family had been making glass since the Middle Ages, it would appear, near Montpellier; spirits, were kept in glass before the benefits of cask ageing were recognised; so were medicines of course. And so the progress of medicines and spirits was followed by these 'gentlemen glassmakers'. The aristocracy was not supposed to indulge in trade, glassmaking being the one exception – a privilege that dates back to the time of Louis IX of France.

Some old bottles of this period are preserved in the *Musée d'Armagnac* in the town of Condom. But again no-one is quite sure whether these were used to keep wine or armagnac in. Just how and when it was realised that armagnac could deteriorate as well as improve in cask, after a certain number of years, remains obscure. Certainly, a trade other than in cask is not known before the 1840s or so, and labels on bottles began around the 1850s. We may perhaps assume that much

*Right: Part of an alambic armagnacais.
Below: 18th-century copper chaudière.
Bottom: An illicit still.*

18th and 19th century bottles from the Musée de l'Armagnac.

larger glass jars or *bonbonnes* as they are known locally, were used for the storage of armagnac as well as wines, at any rate locally, from the mid-eighteenth century onwards. The casks, after all, needed to be re-used for ageing of new wines and/or spirits; few people had the means, or the wood, to afford new ones annually. But shipping in glass jars, much less in bottles, would have been quite impracticable under then prevailing conditions.

But I digress. We must establish the other facts about the internal trade of armagnac before we move onto perhaps the most revealing aspect of my research, foreign trade in armagnac. It is in the mid-eighteenth century that we begin to see the historical factors leading to the establishment of Armagnac as a region with its own *appellation controlée*.

During the reign of Louis XIV the depradations of tax gatherers were at their worst to feed his armies and pay for the extravagances of his court. The early years of Louis XV's reign saw some improvement but not much. Agriculture throughout France was at a low ebb; vines were uprooted to grow the bare necessities of life – in the Armagnac region, mostly maize (today used for fattening geese rather than keeping humans from starvation). Then, suddenly, towards the middle of the eighteenth century, there was a great change. Agriculture was officially recognised as a department of state; the *intendants* (King's commissioners) were charged with seeing that peasant proprietors were protected rather than robbed. Gascony was particularly lucky in d'Etigny, appointed in 1751 and dying in harness (at the early age of 47) after wearing himself out on the King's business. His last letter to the King at Versailles, dated 24 August 1767 is preserved in marble on his statue at Auch. He constructed roads and bridges, encouraged both internal and export trade, introduced manufacturing industries such as tiles and linen as well as encouraging agriculture. "If", he concluded, "I have one regret, it is not to be able to serve Your Majesty longer, or to contribute any more to the well-being of this province . . ." The people of Gascony have not forgotten him or his good works.

He did all he could locally, but the final impulse, as regards communications, came from Turgot in 1776. The long-standing privilege (or monopoly) of Bordeaux was abolished; what is more, in the space of a few years main road arteries from Paris were so much improved that the journey from

A view of the chai at the Domaine Capin, Cazaubon.

Toulouse to the capital was halved, from fourteen to just under seven days. Again, we do not precisely know how this affected the trade in armagnacs, while internal tolls at every town, river and province boundary remained much as they had been. But travel to, and above all through, the region had become very much easier. The best part of Armagnac lay right on the route from Vézeley to the shrine of St Jacques de Compostelle in Spain. (It still does, for that matter, and books are still being written about this pilgrimage.) More pilgrims would now refresh themselves with the wines and spirit of Gascony, on passing through. The pilgrim flask, by the way, bears a strong resemblance to that *basquaise* still preferred by many producers for bottling armagnac.

When we get to the sixteenth century we, or at any rate the Gascons, are on shakier ground. It is claimed that the 'fiery water' from what is referred to as *le haut pays* was then already shipped in large quantities to Bordeaux and thence abroad. But what exactly is *le haut pays*? It could mean way further up country, or high ground. There is much evidence for distilling in the Pyrenees at this time. And the first shipment actually named, in 1513, is from Gaillac, in the Tarn region.

In the seventeenth century, the armagnac trade begins to come into focus. Merchant vessels are known to have cruised down the Bay of Biscay as far as Bayonne and to have shipped quite large quantities of armagnac to Bordeaux, or back to Holland. But from what is known by way of contemporary documentation, this was not then drunk in preference to cognac. Far from it: the Bordeaux merchants used it to fortify the weaker cognacs or to fortify wines. So did the Dutch. Meanwhile, the cognac trade was establishing itself with shipments to England, one such being advertised in the *London Gazette* during the 1680s. A cognac shipper still in existence, Philippe Augier, was founded in 1643. England as a market for armagnac remained an unopened chapter for almost another two centuries.

All the available evidence suggests that armagnac *per se*, and not as a fortifier of other spirits or wines, continued to be enjoyed largely in its region of origin. There were no great *négociant* houses like the Martells or the Hines, which began to spring up in the Cognac region immediately after the death of Louis XIV. When they did spring up, around a century later, they were on a much smaller scale. Communications continued to be a bugbear and armagnac continued to languish in a sort of backwater. It was not until the 1820s that the Baîse became navigable from Nérac up to Lavardac. An extension of the canal as far south as Condom followed in 1839. Now the region was on the map. But the railway did not arrive at Lavardac until 1880, and even today most of the Gers *département* continues to be deprived of it. It is merely encircled by a branch line from Agen to Riscle; and there is a sort of spur out from Toulouse as far as Auch.

In the mid-eighteenth century we at last get an indication that armagnac has found its way to Paris and the court of Louis XV. The Marquis d'Ivry was not only Master of the King's Hunt but also of his table. He owned large estates both around Toulouse and further east: among his known *domaines* were some near Cazaubon, Ayzieu, Mauléon d'Armagnac and Campagne d'Armagnac – still known today as among the best producing areas of the Bas-Armagnac.

The French Revolution, put an end to all that, which is to say, the growing appreciation of armagnac as an up-market product among the Paris aristocracy. But we should remember that not all the French aristocracy was guillotined, and that Gascony is far enough from Paris to have escaped some of the worst excesses. Among those who lived on quietly in the seclusion of their estates was the Marquis de Bonas.

Antoine de Mellet, Marquis de Bonas (1744–1822)

*T*he family of Mellet is one of the most ancient of which we have records in Gascony; their patent of nobility dates back to 1411 – a year which, by an odd coincidence, is also that when a certain Antoine is mentioned as first distiller in Toulouse. It seems apt that another Antoine should put the distinctive Armagnac still finally on the map.

We need not pursue the family's history during earlier centuries, distinguished though it was in civil and military affairs over the years. Suffice it to say that the young Marquis at first followed a military career, too, becoming a captain in the royal cavalry at the age of 25 in 1769. He resigned his commission upon the death of his mother, from whom he inherited the Bonas estate, of which he took charge most probably during the winter of 1781/2 (the precise date remains unknown).

He found the *château* in a bad state of repair, the outbuildings practically in ruins, fields, woodlands and vineyards a jungle, farm implements rusty and needing replacement. His first task was to rebuild the stables – he remained a passionate horseman and huntsman throughout his life; and indeed, horses were vital to him in supervising the rehabilitation of his estate, it was not uncommon for him to wear out a couple of them over twelve hours.

Soon, five pairs of oxen ploughed up the neglected fields, the soil was carefully analysed, and cultivations divided into cereals (mainly wheat) and vines. Both red and white were planted, the latter entirely for distillation. By 1789 all was in fairly fine fettle, the *château*, refurbished and refurnished in splendid style, had become a centre for brilliant receptions with Madame la Marquise as a much appreciated hostess; hunting parties by the river Baïse, which formed the boundary of the estate, and with a *vieux moulin* as hunting-lodge, were other frequent and popular events.

Today's answer; a gleaming copper still.

In brief, a typical pastoral idyll of the *Ancien Régime*. Then came the Revolution, many of his friends emigrated, he himself decided to stay, reducing all pomp and expenditure to a minimum. In 1891, his wife died and he no longer left the estate, concentrating more than ever all his efforts on improving the estate as much as he could. Notably, he was left in peace even during the worst days of the Terror.

His lonely evenings were now given over to reading and study. His studies convinced him to grow more wines, especially white wines for distillation. Leases were granted to his tenants for 29 years on a half share basis of all produce; from 1796 onwards he prospered more and more (and so did those who depended on him). In 1797 he became one of the principal founders of the *Société d'Agriculture du Gers*, which has sought ever since – by way of both theoretical studies and practical advice – to improve the state of agriculture in the Gers *département*.

The structure of this Society allowed for honorary, resident and corresponding members. Of the honorary members, the famous chemist Chaptal (also Minister of the Interior), Lacapède and Parmentier, all resident in Paris, were the most eminent.

That same year, with the harvest better than ever, the Marquis decided that a new building was necessary for both storage of wine and distillation. He used for this purpose two existing outbuildings, standing parallel to each other but twelve metres apart. The empty space between them was filled in, and there resulted a new building 24 metres square and ten high. What had previously been merely crude barns used as stables and for fodder now became known as *l'Atelier*, the working heart of the entire estate.

Antoine himself was what the French call *un physiocarte*: an aristocrat whose hobby or even passion was science, and especially the sciences of physics and chemistry. Dissatisfied with the results he was obtaining in distillation, he corresponded with, among others, Chaptal.

It was thus that he heard of a then new still, invented by Adam in 1801. He lost little time in installing this, the forerunner of what was to become the traditional Armagnac continuous still, on his estate. Obviously, it was some years before the news spread that here was a new method, which as well as being cheaper and simpler to operate than the older (Charentais) double-distillation type, also produced a liquor

Traditional grape press from the Armagnac region.

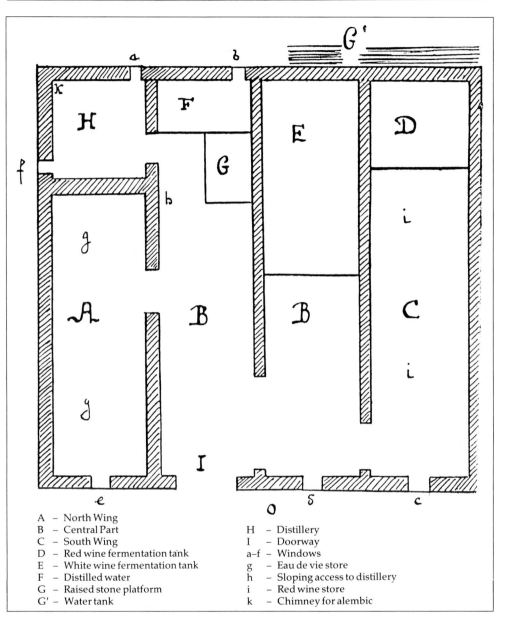

A – North Wing
B – Central Part
C – South Wing
D – Red wine fermentation tank
E – White wine fermentation tank
F – Distilled water
G – Raised stone platform
G' – Water tank

H – Distillery
I – Doorway
a–f – Windows
g – Eau de vie store
h – Sloping access to distillery
i – Red wine store
k – Chimney for alembic

The family de Bonas was in the forefront of armagnac production. The plan above shows their carefully thought out distillerie and chai. of much higher-flavoured character. As this quality began to be appreciated, other experiments followed; and by the 1820s a number of makers of such new stills had established themselves in the region, at Eauze, Agen and other places.

It is from here that we can really trace the origins of what we know as armagnac today, a spirit produced by a single distillation as opposed to the double distillation of the Cognac region.

67

L'Alembic Armagnacais

*T*he elements that go to making a beautiful and individual brandy are many and varied, but perhaps there are some which are more important than others. The quality of the wine before it is distilled is determined by the soil, the grape, the sun and the rain. The character of the distilled spirit is affected by the wood of the barrels, the way and the length of time that it is stored before being put in bottles. And just as there must be an initiation of any boy before he becomes a man, so there must be a baptism by fire of the wine before it becomes a spirit.

The principle upon which the science of distillation is based is that alcohol becomes vapour at 78.3 degrees centigrade, thus allowing the artist to use the tools of science to separate just enough alcohol from the water in the wine to cool it and to determine the strength of the resulting spirit. It is said that the Arabs were the first to learn how to distil, that they introduced the skill into Europe through Spain, but that the science only became an art when it crossed the Pyrenees into France.

The summit of the art of distilling wine is the pot still which is retained in Armagnac and Cognac. The patent stills, in which gin, grain whisky, vodka and some other brandies are distilled, are more efficient in that they offer a process which produces a neutral spirit, harmonious yet devoid of idiosyncrasies. It is worth noting that malt whiskies with their individualities are the products of pot stills.

Until the early nineteenth century there was little difference between the distillation methods of Armagnac and Cognac, but the tradition slowly evolved that cognac should be distilled twice (that tradition is now enshrined in law) whereas armagnac should be distilled but once. And the reason why such a difference emerged was the development of the *Alembic Armagnacais*.

In 1801, a chemist in Montpellier, Edouard Adam, invented a still that was portable enough to be moved from farm to farm – and if anything ever appeals to the Gascon it is something which enables him to be independent. By 1850 the still had been perfected by Monsieur Verdier and the individual farmer was now no longer beholden to the organised production houses which had begun to spring up. In 1835 there were upwards of fifty or sixty such houses, but by the turn of the century there were less than ten (now reduced to six or seven). Mind you, they still account for at least two thirds of all armagnac sales.

The *alembic armagnacais* produces brandy in a shorter time than the traditional pot still; it uses less wine – 100 litres of wine yield 20 litres of spirit; it distils at a lower temperature and the spirit leaves the still at between 50–55° volume, as opposed to 70° from the pot still. Thus a great deal more

An old alembic ambulant graces Janneau's headquarters in Condom.

character of the original wine survives; there is a lot more scope for individuality; a less standard product emerges.

It is in the winter that the wine is distilled. The fermentation of the wine is completed by the turn of the year and the producer turns to his still or awaits the arrival of the itinerant distiller with his apparatus. Today there are very few *alembics ambulants*, because most producers now have their own stills, but it would be wrong to say that they have died out completely.

Here I wish to quote from the great Joseph de Pesquidoux, a writer, perhaps the greatest of all writers, a son of the soil, a producer and a lover of armagnac.

> 'Today there are still ambulating alembics which burn and distil our wines. They arrive on high, two-wheeled carts. They are then installed under a shed, sheltered from the wind. They engulf the wine like unfathomable chasms.
>
> 'The flame is the soul of the distillation. When it is too ardent it gives to the *eau de vie* what is called *le coup de feu* or as we should say in English, the taste and characteristic of having been burnt. It emerges from that experience harsh, virulent, corrosive. On the other hand when the blaze is lacking in ardour, it gives an *eau de vie* without strength or consistency. The quality of the flame depends upon that of the wood. The latter must be dry, non resinous, capable of being entirely and completely consumed. The finest and best combustible is a mixture of powerful and yet gentle alder wood and oak.
>
> 'So families from father to son follow this trade of wine-burners. They proceed experimentally. One drop of the spirit as it leaves the alembic, and rolled on their tongue and they will tell you "I have distilled at such and such a degree". When their apparatus is installed in mid-autumn these men work in twelve-hour shifts. Like soldiers they eat and drink without leaving their work. With the night they take on a typical aspect, going and coming in front of the alembic, enveloped in a blanket or rug. They are aloof and apart from the world. They scarcely lift their eyes to look at the round pure moon. They scarcely give an ear to the sudden

barking of a dog or the short hooting of a hunting owl.

The heart and soul of 'farmagnac'.

'As a little child then I haunted the *chai* on distillation nights. I have known a renowned 'burner' operating on all our estates. One had to book up a year in advance in order not to lose one's turn for the distillation. He arrived punctually; his feet in straw-lined wooden sabots, dressed warmly with a woollen girdle to protect his kidneys from night-cold and a shawl or rug around his shoulders. Silently he saluted and at once took his place beside the alembic. And then he commenced work.

'He was called *Meste Jean* (or Master John) in order to indicate, and in recognition of his incomparable fashion of 'burning' or distilling the wine. There was no need of any family name. Master John sufficed. I verily believe that all the countryside heard and knew his slow and slightly heavy step. Whilst he was at his distillation no one could get a word from him. All his being was engrossed in the noise of the wine which bubbled or boiled above the consuming wood. He had the air of listening with the whole of his being; his eyes half-closed, those eyes that the constantly watched and supervised flame had turned to a pale blue.'

The rustic sight of the ambulant alembic is now more frequently to be seen in old engravings than in reality, but the ensuing development whereby each proprietor has come to possess his own alembic is no less awesome – a huge installation bricked into a corner of the wine vault with its patinated copper plates.

Young de Pesquidoux would slip away immediately after the evening meal to the *chai* where he would stand and wait for that moment when the furnace door was thrown open to project a red golden glare across the hogshead casks 'giving to the range of monstrous vats the aspect of hills on fire'.

The magic of armagnac is derived from those mysterious moments. Imagine the scene with the producer, his children, his chickens and his barrels lit in the strange light of leaping red flames from a dry wood fire. And deny if you can that the resulting spirit must have qualities denied to the product of the clinical distillation plants of the large producers.

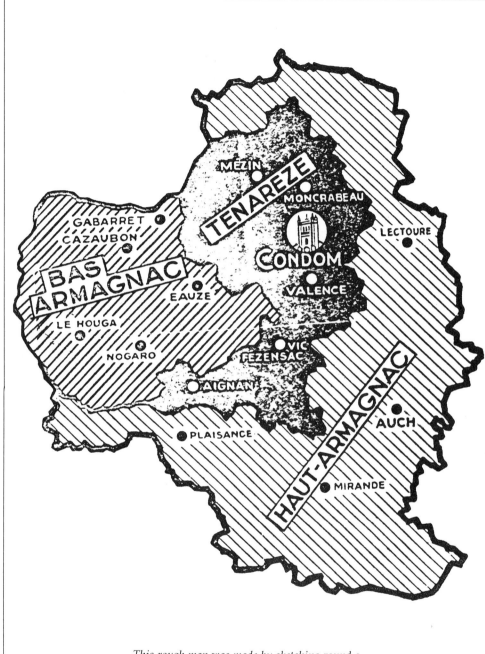

*This rough map was made by sketching round a
vine leaf which proved to be just the right shape.*

Soil Variations

The soil must be thoroughly prepared, as in this case, for propagation of ugni blanc.

A map of the Armagnac region looks for all the world like a vine leaf – a nice coincidence. A closer look will show up a network of rivers, almost fan-shaped. The river Adour and its two or three small tributaries form the western 'link' of this open fan; the Garonne, where it turns sharply at Toulouse towards the Pyrenees, its eastern link. All the other rivers watering the region, such as Save, Gers and Baïse, are tributaries of the Garonne and flow more or less due south.

I include the eastern half here, although nowadays the river Gers forms more or less the limits of armagnac production.

The combination of soil and grape is the start of the process which will lead to M. Dauriac's excellent armagnac many years later.

42° vol.   70cl.

armagnac
Dauriac

APPELLATION **BAS ARMAGNAC** CONTROLEE

A.M DAURIAC & Fils

PROPRIETAIRE   RECOLTANT

DOMAINE de "GASTON" • LANNEPAX • 32190-VIC-FEZENSAC

FRANCE

Indeed, it is rare even east of the Baïse. In earlier centuries, however, spirit was distilled here too, and in some quantity. What sort of spirit we do not quite know: we read of the *picpoul nègre*, a red-wine variety which is not among those authorised today.

The configuration of the land and its soil go back far into prehistoric times, the tertiary period, when all this part of south-west France was under water. When the land rose owing to volcanic and other upheavals which we need not describe here, rivers and valleys formed as we know them today. But when the ocean withdrew it left very different kinds of debris and sediment in different parts. Not always regularly: there are outcrops of various soils, even sandy ones, not only in the Landes but much further east. It was only gradually realised that the best soil for growing armagnac-producing vines lay in a part roughly west of Eauze. In fact, during a nineteenth century attempt to classify the regions (vy. Seillan, in the 1860s) Eauze itself was mapped as being within the Ténarèze.

Grape Varieties

'*F*ings ain't wot they used to be' . . . Writing around 1947, the late Joseph de Pesquidoux, a great writer of the Armagnac region, describes the composition of a pre-phylloxera armagnac as half *piquepoult* (*folle blanche* in modern terms) a quarter Jurançon or Muscat and a quarter *oeil de Fourde*. The last was a purely local plant which has now died out, and so called because it resembled the eye of a bird with that local name. At that time, Pesquidoux still had a few old bottles; when he offered some drops to a local taster, the latter removed his beret, saying "one must drink this uncovered!" Such was the quality of what Pesquidoux himself called 'this unique essence'.

Throughout the nineteenth century, grape varieties were largely uncontrolled (by official bodies, I mean); it was not until the limits of Armagnac were fixed by the decree of 1909 that it was thought advisable to allow and recommend certain vines for armagnac production and prohibit others. The recommended varieties today are: *Baco 22A*, *Clairette*, *Colombard*, *Folle blanche*, *Graisse*, *Mauzac blanc*, *Meslier St François* and *Ugni blanc*. Permitted in addition to these are the *Jurançon blanc* and *St Emilion*.

When we come to look at the distribution of these varieties, we find that the *Baco 22A* is limited largely to the '*sables fauves*' areas of the Bas-Armagnac and a very small part of the north-western Ténarèze, where the soil may be similar. Again, the *folle blanche* is limited to the better part of Bas-Armagnac, towards the Landes. More than two-thirds of the region is planted with *ugni blanc*, though there has been a shift towards some of the rarer and more delicate varieties once more over the past ten years.

Today, the *ugni blanc* dominates to the extent of over 50% mainly because of its hardiness and reliability. But this again is not altogether satisfactory, except to those who favour

'cognarm' in any case, as it is basically the same grape as that which produces cognac in the Charente. What individuality it maintains once distilled comes from the soil rather than from the grape. It certainly gains from being mixed – either at vinification stage or during distillation, with a more aromatic wine, say *mauzac* or Jurançon. The proportions will, of course, vary from grower to grower and blender from blender, and from Ténarèze to Bas-Armagnac according to the nature of the soil.

Harvesting the grapes in the Bas-Armagnac.

I have referred to the hardiness of this plant; but now a new danger looms in the form of a fungus called *'eutypiose'*, a fungus which attacks the vine at the point where it is pruned and can then spread through to the root. While not as quick in murder as was the phylloxera, it can still destroy a previously healthy vine within six to ten years. There is at the moment no known cure for this blight, first discovered in France during 1977 and now gradually spreading south; already it is affecting some 4% of the *cabernet sauvignon* crop, while in the Cognac region some 20% of vines are now probably affected. Whether or when it will reach the Armagnac region is not yet certain; maybe some new chemical spray will be found before it does. Nor is it known whether it affects all vines equally; but the *ugni blanc* is definitely under threat.

Given proper care, the *folle blanche* or *piquepoult* produces the most aromatic spirit. It tends to need constant supervision and nursing, being particularly susceptible to both botrytis (the grey rot which attacks vine leaves) and black-rot, which attacks the grapes themselves. Frequent and costly spraying is involved to help keep these at bay; you might say that the *folle blanche* demands nursing rather than just care. Yet there are growers like Monsieur Léon Lafitte of Le Frèche who has consecrated about one-third of his acreage to this difficult plant, vinfies, distills and bottles it separately, and has made a big success of it in international markets (again, we seem to lag behind in the UK). There is a compensation in another way too: the *folle blanche* liquor matures rather more rapidly than others, nearing perfection already at ten years old.

Monsieur Lafitte's also separately vinified and distilled *colombard* is almost as appreciated by connoisseurs in and beyond the region as his *folle blanche*. But it must be said that this is an exception, as Monsieur Lafitte is an exceptional grower/distiller. Generally speaking, the *colombard* is used in blends; by itself, it does much better as a white wine, which has found its way to England via the *Caves du Saint-Mont* in the Landes. In the Armagnac region, it lags well behind *ugni blanc* and *Baco 22A*.

The same applies to the other grape varieties here shown; one might be tempted not to mention them at all, except that they are still grown in small quantities and favoured for blending by particular growers. Generally speaking, they are

*A promising bunch of folle blanche, which is
limited to Bas-Armagnac and the Landes.*

too high in alcohol and sugar, and lack the necessary acidity for good distilling – at any rate on their own. They flourish mostly in the Ténarèze, especially near Montréal, where Veuve Ladevèze has some Jurançon vines over 50 years old and still yielding. She also has some *plant de graisse*; again, her success – she wins gold medals regularly for her produce – is due to her skilful blending, the result being complex aromas not easily found elsewhere.

Other varieties are fast disappearing altogether. Monsieur Lafitte is said to grow a little *mauzac* (the principal grape of the Gaillac region), but too little to matter much; the small percentage he may add to his blends remains his secret. The *mauzac* is really a wine grape, not very suitable for distilling; it is known also as *blanquette* and, further south, produces what is perhaps the best sparkler outside Champagne – *Blanquette de Limoux*, in the Languedoc.

BAS ARMAGNAC

APPELLATION BAS ARMAGNAC CONTROLÉE

COMTE de GUYON

1965   48% vol

Maupas en Armagnac 32240 Estang (Gers)

PRODUCE OF FRANCE   1,5 L

The Ageing Process

Here we had best forget about the old adage that the exception proves the rule; here there are no rules, only exceptions. The Gascon is never more individualistic than in the way he uses his casks.

I am talking of traditional black oak casks, from the forest of Monlezun, not of 'cognarm' ones imported from the Limousin or elsewhere. The textbook ritual says 'a year or two in new oak of 400 litres, then transfer to large used vats.' This scarcely ever happens; hence the almost infinite variety of armagnacs. Some producers never use new oak; some never transfer from cask to vat but believe it best to let the spirit rest unperturbed for 30 years or so. In 1904, Joseph Laberdolive, father of Gérard and grandfather of the present owner Pierre, had the bright idea of putting his whole year's distillation into a huge vat holding 10,000 litres. (Even the locals thought he had gone out of his mind.) It stayed there for 53 years and is reckoned to be one of the best you can buy. Similarly, Monsieur Théaux of the *Domaine Sans*, leaves his 1935 in cask still, unless someone asks for a bottle. Up the road at Cazeneuve, at *La Pouche*, Monsieur Morel does not believe in new casks at all; his armagnacs go straight into used ones. Others again may say anything from three to six years in new oak, and who am I to argue with them . . .?

It depends partly on the manner of your distilling, partly on the nature of the *chai*, partly on the 'nose' of the producer and on what he has found to be best over the years. And, of course, the actual harvest of grapes being distilled. In the end, there are still unexplained differences from cask to cask, both perhaps of the same age and distillation. Which is why a restaurateur like Daguin of the *Hotel de France* at Auch hand-picks his casks, according to his individual taste. And on his bottles specifies *'pièce choisie par André Daguin'* – without specifying the particular property where he bought it! For he

Cooper at work. may well have bought the cask some years ago, so that –
though now twenty years old – it was further matured in his
cellars and is now, quite genuinely, a Daguin armagnac, not
that of Mr X.

If there is more of a regular pattern, I have still to discover it.
If you want an armagnac that tastes the same year-in, year-out,
best stick to a brand by one of the large shippers.

Years ago, in the second edition of his *World Atlas of Wine*,
Hugh Johnson wrote that if you aged armagnac in casks from
the Limousin or Tronçais forests (as used for maturing
cognac) you got something which was neither cognac nor
armagnac. I note that he no longer says so in the third edition:
were there perhaps protests from the growing 'cognarm'
brigade?

Your 'farmagnac' producer will certainly be adamant that only the local oak will do: that dark oak which comes from the forest of Monlezun, or from what they actually call (as an area) *L'Armagnac Noir*, in the Landes, just before oak trees give way to pines.

I fear the wood of this cask is too light to have come from Monlezun.

You will see from the table opposite that this oak has a slightly different chemical composition to that from forests further north.

COMPOSITION DE DIFFÉRENTS BOIS DE CHÊNE

	Lignine	Tanins	Vanilline	Syringal-déhyde	Coniféral-déhyde
Tronçais	56.5	105.3	1.85	1.75	0.68
Limousin	57.0	87.0	3.62	4.00	1.23
Gascogne	55.0	114.0	3.23	3.48	0.83

And this chemical composition obviously affects the way in which the spirit matures. For one thing, the greater richness in tannin content helps to give a richer colour sooner – that deep amber colour which is a characteristic of armagnacs. Your armagnac farmer will allow no addition of sugar, caramel or any other substance; all must proceed naturally with the lapse of time. And that may be anything from ten to fifteen years in the Bas-Armagnac, where the spirit is less harsh even as it runs from the still into the cask, to twenty or more years in the Ténarèze.

Which is, of course, one of the reasons why a really good Ténarèze unblended and unadulterated, is just as expensive as a good Bas-Armagnac. I would say that any difference is not of quality but of kind: your expert will detect more of a scent of violets here than of prunes. Soil and grape varieties play their part, too. The very sandy soil of the Grand Bas favours the *Baco 22A*, a hybrid which is hardy and gives the most delicate brandy – apart from perhaps, the *folle blanche*, which, owing to its extreme fragility, and the constant care it needs, accounts for less than 1% of total production.

At what age you find an armagnac drinkable depends entirely on your palate – and of course on your purse. I am sorry, in a way, that the BNIA has officially adopted the cognac method of grading, which is largely meaningless. VSOP (very superior old pale) may mean anything from three years up (with often, admittedly, a shot of something much older to help give a good blend); and the large *négoçiants* depend on a fairly large and rapid turnover. But the very term VSOP creates a confusion as to what a fine armagnac is all about. If it is very superior old then it certainly will not be pale! Of course this, too, is a generalisation, as different grape varieties and blends give different shades of colour. But basically it would be true to say that 'pale' is a sign of quality in some of the best cognacs (e.g. Delamain Pale and Dry, or early-landed/late bottled cognacs matured here in damp Bristol or London cellars to particular – or, as the French think – peculiar – English tastes, often <u>below</u> 40° vol); whereas the opposite is true of a fine armagnac: it fills the room with the pungency of its perfume as soon as you open the bottle, and it is by no means pale either in colour or alcoholic strength.

Vintages

Another drawback of armagnac is that the local authorities have adopted the cognac scale of ageing, from 00 for a spirit one year in cask to 6 (*hors d'age*), after which specific ages or vintages must be stated. There was, until very recently, one difference: vintage cognacs were not officially allowed except in export markets (e.g. early-landed and bottled much later in UK). Subject to strict supervision, however, vintages may now be declared in the Cognac region once more. It would seem, therefore, that one of the principal advantages of armagnac over cognac has gone. But was it really so much of an advantage? Or – to put it another way – were people really fooled? Or – to put it quite brusquely – if they were, should they have been?

Spirits, unlike wines, mature in cask, not in bottle. Again, unlike wine, they may rapidly deteriorate in bottle if some idiot stores them horizontally rather than vertically. The contact of cork and spirits is as injurious as contact of cork and wine is beneficial.

Thus that great 1893 Armagnac vintage, for which certain merchants who should know better ask £200+ per bottle, is likely to be at best a small disappointment and at worst a great 'con'. Of course, it can be a supreme delight, but only if you have the answers to the following questions: (1) how old were the vines from which the armagnac was made? and what vines were they? (2) how long was the armagnac matured in cask? (3) how and where was it subsequently stored?

That pedigree is not generally forthcoming – so I can only here say "beware!". There are far too many of these 1893s around for my liking, which may, for all we know, have been bottled around 1903/4, and whose corks may be thoroughly corroded. The practice of using sealing-wax liberally (instead of a plain tinfoil capsule) looks pretty but disguises any defects even better. So does opaque or green glass.

Three-star and VSOP are largely meaningless. The first is perhaps best used for cooking, or pouring into an espresso. The latter may mean almost anything, but is very rarely a 'very superior old pale', certainly nothing like what we tend to associate with Delamain's Pale and Dry cognac! (I am told, and I can quite believe it, that this consists of exclusively Grande Champagne cognac, all over fifteen years old and some over twenty-five.)

Testing the spirit. Don't let the demijohns (bonbonnes) mislead you. In Cognac they are used for old brandy which becomes 'woody' if left in barrel for too long.

What, then should you be looking for in armagnac? If a vintage, certainly a bottle which states the date of bottling as

well as distilling. Thus a 1966 bottled in 1986 will have spent twenty years in cask and should be appropriately full-bodied and amber-coloured. For – contrary to cognacs – colour comes with age – at least when the spirit is kept in local oak, which is darker and has more tannin than that of the Tronçais or Limousin regions, favoured for cognac.

But I have my doubts about vintages, too. To what extent are they really meaningful, given all the other factors which go into the making of a great brandy? We know, indeed, that we do not want good wine grapes; we need low alcoholic content

91

A complete cross-section from 3-star, VSOP, Hors d'Age and Tres Vieux to Vintage.

and high acidity as an ideal distilling product. In some years, when conditions are far from ideal, the better armagnac producers will not distil at all but turn their grapes over to the local *cave co-opérative* to make wine. A good, hot summer, with grapes heavy with sugar, is often a bad summer for distilling them later.

So again: be suspicious of vintages – and especially of producers who declare a vintage every year. This is strictly for the Japanese or USA markets, where vintages have become all the rage.

A much surer guide to quality is the stated age without specific vintage. If a bottle says *15 ans,* that means that the youngest armagnac in that bottle must have spent at least fifteen years in cask; and, maybe, has some older armagnacs added to it, to give it extra 'body' and flavour. Here you are on sure ground, as with single malt whiskies – and even certain blends. A whisky whose bottle proclaims '12 years old' is always at least that age, and may well have some older whiskies in it. Such is the law, rigorously enforced; and such is also the law throughout Armagnac.

The comparison with single malt whiskies seems to me the more apposite in that there are around 120 distinct ones, as against thousands of blends. Each has, for reasons as yet scientifically undetermined, its own peculiar character (some like Talisker or Laphroaig – more peculiar than others, and an acquired taste). But cognoscenti will tell an Islay from a Highland malt without difficulty; and if you prefer a Campbeltown or an Orkney malt, who is to say you nay? This variety (the spice of life) is part of their charm and endless fascination. Thus it is with armagnacs once you get to know and appreciate them. They, too, thrive best aged in cask for between ten and twenty-five years; and they, too, may benefit from having older ones added to those more youthful.

Which leads me on to over-ageing. I have heard it said that very old armagnacs, 40 years on or so, cannot be told apart – even by expert tasters – from very old and fine rums, cognacs or malt whiskies. If that be so, I would ask: what is the point? Especially as you probably have to pay through the nose for such spirits. For my own part, my motto remains *Vive la différence*.

I have already hinted how differences in methods of ageing, and of casks used, may affect the character of different armagnacs – or even of armagnacs from one and the same distillation. Within the small village of Cazeneuve, for instance, you will find half a dozen producers following their own pet theories – all the way from keeping an armagnac in new wood throughout its life to putting it straight into large old barrels. In between, you will find those who believe in two, three or five years in brand-new casks. There are those who will fuss over the spirit and those who believe in leaving it undisturbed. The nature of the *chai*, its ventilation and humidity, exposure to the elements, wooden, concrete or earthen floor – all of these play some part. When it comes to blended armagnacs, what is called the *coupage* or *assemblage*, again there are almost as many different opinions as producers. If you are growing four different grape varieties, do you distil them separately or together? And, if you distil them separately, at what age is it best to blend? Please do not ask me for definitive answers to these questions: once again, the proof of the spirit is in the drinking and savouring of it.

There is also *le rancio*. This should not be taken to mean rancid, but a very delicate sweetness that has nothing sugary or syrupy about it. And, again, it is only to be found in armagnacs distilled and matured in the traditional manner. I say drinking and savouring, because that is what a good *digestif* is all about. That very word implies a settling of the stomach, to

the benefit of the meal which has gone before. Yes, you may sniff first, but in the end you must swallow. The spittoon has, happily, no place in armagnac tastings. The warmth which you feel first upon your palate should spread itself throughout your system.

A good armagnac should be perfectly round and smooth and have no trace of harshness. A hint of fieriness, perhaps, even in old ones, yet nothing that catches you at the back of the throat. One of the surprising facts about the best old armagnac, maybe 48° alcohol content, is that it does not seem all that alcoholic, maybe less so than one that has been reduced to just 40° by means of distilled water. Since all its elements are in complete harmony, since it is perfectly balanced, there is simply nothing to disturb. It has also what the local experts call *le gras*. The last thing this implies is greasiness or oiliness: merely a slightly thicker texture or overall composition than you would sense if it has been diluted with water. Water thins, there is no getting away from

it. Thus you may compare the difference between a true, barrel-proof armagnac and a reduced one with the difference between a perfume (*essence*) and an *eau-de-toilette*. The comparison is the more apt because both are distilled spirits. And just as we talk of the 'essential oils' in perfumes, so they exist in armagnacs.

You can, of course, distil them right out, by repeated and high-temperature distillations. You then have what is called a 'neutral' spirit – which is precisely what a good armagnac is not. The single distillation at a fairly low proof strength (52° to 58° alcohol) ensures that what are professionally called the *congenerics* remain. The balanced flavours of these are only brought out by long maturing in oak casks. But the initial balance must be there, the nastier flavours expelled – wherein lies the art of the distiller.

Termes d'Armagnac, a 14th-century, fortified tower residence, restored and used today as a local history museum.

A country church near Eauze, the very heart of the Armagnac region.

Armagnac vintage in full swing.

A vineyard and small manor house, typical of the Bas-Armagnac region.

Testing the grapes for ripeness.

Despite its stubborn individualism, Armagnac moves with the times as the mechanical harvester goes to work.

Larressingle, one of the many bastides, or fortified villages, that bear testimony to Gascony's rugged history.

Fuelling an old armagnac still for the traditional, low-temperature, single distillation.

A tonnellier at work, binding the seasoned oak staves to create the armagnac cask.

The black oaks of the Monzelun forest are vital to armagnac's strong, rustic flavour.

Tasting armagnac in an old chai, direct from the cask, where the vital ageing process occurs.

Armagnac and Cognac

*P*erhaps we should look at basic differences from cognac a little more closely. I have no wish at all to denigrate cognac here: I like it too much. And comparisons, as Dogberry reminds us, are 'odorous'.

The malapropism, for once, is apt. You test the main difference first and foremost by smell rather than by taste – or as wine trade jargon would have it, by the nose rather than the palate. For very good reasons do Cognac folk call the best of their blends, from Grande and Petite Champagne regions, *Fine Champagne*. There is, or should be, about them first and foremost a certain delicacy. There is also, at any rate in England, a preference for the 'pale and dry'. It is a fastidious drink, seldom offered at over 40° vol strength; and ladies enjoy it as much as do gentlemen.

By contrast, great armagnacs are round, full and pungent, and should retain, even into old age (twenty years or more is not uncommon) a hint of that fieriness I have already referred to. I would say that it is, like vintage port, very much a man's drink. It is a favourite when men are by themselves, perhaps after a *grand diner de chasse* – males talking about male pursuits like hunting the boar or shooting pigeons (both much practised in the region). Few such men would deem it worthwhile to take an in any way diluted postprandial drink. Their *digestif* will be powerful: they will maintain the tradition that no good armagnac is ever reduced by the addition of distilled water. It will be served at barrel-proof (and most likely straight from the cask of one among their company), at whatever strength the owner deems it is at its best. This may well be as much as 57° vol and is hardly likely to be less than 43° vol.

This is, maybe, also one of the reasons why armagnac has not made as much impact on international markets as cognac.

Above: Cognac from the bottle.
Below: Armagnac from the barrel.

It is always easier to sell a standardised product than one which varies as much as does armagnac. The names of the regions do not exactly help. Everyone can appreciate the meaning of *'grande'* or *'fine'* (Cognac). Who is to know, without being told, that *'Bas'* (Armagnac) does not mean low in quality but refers merely to the lie of the land? Some producers I know do not use the word *Bas* for that reason, though entitled to it; others have invented a largely fictitious and quite unofficial *'Grand Bas'*. Whether this helps boost their product or merely confuses the public further is a moot point.

Armagnac or cognac? Can you spot the tell-tale signs?

You might also draw a parallel with the contrast between what happens in Bordeaux and Burgundy. One has, especially in the Médoc, large estates, the other many more and smaller, fragmented properties, some of just a hectare or so. The wine trade in Burgundy is similarly much more fragmented. And many small producers are taking to selling their own wine bottled on the property, rather than trusting in large *négoçiants*. The latter may know more about good blending; but the trend nowadays is more and more to *domaine*-bottled wines with their own '*goût de terroir*'. (Which means, in simple terms, keeping the particular flavour of one's own soil and grapes).

Soil and grapes are, of course paramount, and we shall have to look at them in much more detail later. Enough to stress here that whereas in the Cognac region, chalky soil is the best, in Armagnac it is sand. Which brings us to one unique feature of certain parts of the Bas-Armagnac. The dread phylloxera louse does not like sandy soil, whereas the *folle blanche* vine (called *piquepoult* locally) likes it very much. So it happened that some ungrafted, pre-phylloxera vines survived in Armagnac into the 1940s. The yield from such old vines, dating back to the late nineteenth century, was of course very small; and the quantity of distilled spirits now remaining is smaller still. The odd old bottle, if found, might be worth mortgaging your house for . . . a most fantastic bouquet, less fire now than glowing embers perhaps, and incredibly smooth and rich. Forty years in cask would have reduced this to 40° vol strength, or even less; so the ladies may safely join in the pleasure of drinking it. I can imagine no better Golden Wedding gift.

But more of all this when we look at the three main regions of Armagnac in detail.

M. Grassa is known in England also for his côte de Gasgogne wines.

Armagnac and Burgundy

'You may drink Armagnac after Burgundy
and they wont quarrel.'

*T*he comparison with Burgundy, which I made earlier by way of the Saintsbury quotation, could be stretched. For instance, both Burgundy and Armagnac have many small growers rather than large estates. There is also a multiplicity of micro-climates and soils that affect the quality of wines produced (of course, 'quality' means something very different in the two regions, the best wines for distilling armagnac being relatively low in alcohol and sugar). Again, a minority of the very many growers in both regions bottle and sell their own produce: Burgundy has some 140 *négociant* firms, Armagnac 80, which in both cases may or may not own vineyards but try chiefly to produce acceptable blends. Yet in both cases, too, some of the smallest growers make the most sought-after produce. I recall Mr Penning-Rowsell writing of one such who came top of a Montrachet tasting (August 1988 in the *Financial Times*): Monsieur Gagnard, who made precisely two hogshead of his wine – that is to say, 50 cases or 600 bottles . . . !

No wonder prices are, as Mr Penning-Rowsell commented, 'shockingly high' for the best burgundies. But here the comparison ends, for he was writing of 1985 burgundies, just being offered for sale, at anything between £15 and £50 per bottle. No three-year-old armagnac will cost you anything like that. Indeed, you would be hard put to it to find a grower to sell you one at this age: any responsible producer would wish to mature it for ten or even fifteen years before parting with it. We should remember, too, that it takes five litres of wine to distil one litre of armagnac. Given these facts, a fifteen-year-old at £15 or so must be reckoned a great bargain, and you should not begrudge £30 per bottle for one from a small and choice estate in the best region. The number of measures you get out of it will depend, of course, on the generosity of the measures you pour; but it should not be less than seventeen as against six glasses of wine from a bottle of burgundy. If anyone begrudges the cost of that, let them stick to ordinary grape brandies, some of which are fairly tolerable. Or, indeed, a VSOP cognac of doubtful provenance.

Dry (or wet?) Statistics

*I*t was, I think, Disraeli who gave it as his opinion that "there are lies, damned lies, and statistics." I am therefore not at all sure how to treat those which reached me in late October 1988 from the BNIA at Eauze, covering the years 1978–1987, and in some instances going back to the year 1976/7.

From an examination of the figures received, I note that the UK is ahead of all other countries as regards the import of bottled spirits during the year 1986/7, and that the UK runs second overall in export markets. Of the 1,789 hectolitres imported, only a negligible 15 hectolitres were in cask. For this same most recent year, Germany leads overall by a wide margin; but very much less than half of all armagnacs sent to this particular export market was in bottle: only 1,152 hectolitres as against 2,455 hectolitres in cask. Germany lies only in third place as regards bottled imports. Japan shares with the UK a preference for the bottled spirit; but there was a fairly steep decline in overall imports compared with the previous year. On the other hand, Hong Kong sales were up by over 80%, and all of this (in both years) is shown as bottles, no casks at all. The same is true of the USA, though here a decline (albeit slight) is to be noted. Most interesting, perhaps of all is Sweden: in fourth place overall, but not figuring in the bottled table at all. Other points to notice are that Belgium is sixth and Switzerland nowhere.

How much or how little do these figures tell us about the popularity of armagnac in different countries? It is very difficult to say – or at least, to say precisely what kinds of armagnac. Young or old, armagnac or cognac still, *domaine*-bottled or *négociant*/co-op cellar? A breakdown of the UK markets shows one-third Janneau, riding high on Martell's back; the rest is fragmented. I suspect that both Japan and the USA, and not forgetting Hong Kong, tend to look much more up-market – to vintages even. As for the Germans, I am highly suspicious as to what may happen to all those casks they import. I would say that at least some of them go to improving their own many brandies.

The French themselves drink practically half the bottled armagnac that is produced. Or rather, did so during 1986/7. However, you will note a fairly rapid decline in their consumption from 1982/3 onwards – and in fact almost exactly 4,000 hectolitres less than in 1979/80. This decrease in French consumption has not been made up by a corresponding increase in exports; these are seen to have been at a peak during 1978/9 and 1979/80. The total of bottles exported was in 1986/7 still almost 500 hectolitres less than in 1977/8. The % figures that summarise these tables are perhaps the most interesting (and disconcerting?) of all. I mean, in the way that the bottled as against cask product rose from 51.98% to 73.71% (maximum achieved in 1983/4), and has since dropped back again to 65.13%.

What, if anything, does all of this prove? Possibly again that 'crisis of identity' to which I have already referred. Not so long ago (not five years, in fact) the BNIA was trying to promote

The oldest armagnac house still trading, founded by Pascal Dartigalongue at Nogaro.

BAS-ARMAGNAC
CROIX DE SALLES

TREPOT DE LA CROIX DE SALLES

J. DARTIGALONGUE

Photo prise en 1910

de Père en Fils depuis 1838

armagnac as a drink for all occasions, as a mixer even. Lighter spirits, white spirits even, were all the fashion. If you confuse the public, you must expect confusing statistics. I am glad to see that this trend (or trendiness) seems to be over. The most recent utterance by Monsieur Jean-Louis Martin, the present Director of BNIA, is uncompromising on this theme: "Armagnac is not a mixer product. We are in the market of fine spirits, to be taken as *digestifs* at the end of a meal." I have noted, too, that in the most recent publicity brochure for armagnac there is no mention of the Charentais still; only the local one is shown and explained. Perhaps 'cognarm' is on the way out . . . ?

But I anticipate; there remain other tables and statistics to look at. Perhaps the most remarkable is that showing the area of armagnac production. This has shrunk from 21,650 hectares in 1979 to 10,969 hectares in 1987. The most notable shrinkage (or uprooting of vines) has taken place in the Lot-et-Garonne *département*, where the area is down from 1,105 hectares to 409, now less than 40% of what it was.

The distillation table makes the oddest reading of all: up and down like a yoyo. Obviously, with the shrinkage of vineyard area, there has been a drop in distillation too: but this has not, except in the freak years, been too noticeable. Or rather one might say, skilled new agricultural methods have led to better yields: the vineyard area may have been halved, but wines distilled have risen. Whether this is, in the long run, a good or a bad thing, it is too early to judge: high yields may entail a drop in quality. Older vines, too, tend to be better than young ones.

I find the table concerning stocks in some ways rather encouraging. Total stocks stand at seven times the 1987 distillation, somewhat less as regards overall sales for 1986/7. The encouraging feature is the way in which producer's stocks have risen, from 50,691 hectolitres in 1976 to 97,579 hectolitres in 1987. In other words, the estates are stocking up, even saving. Conversely, the co-ops have halved their stocks, and the *négoçiants* are down by almost one-third. Professional distillers, it will be seen, also sold some stock, though fairly insignificant in relation to other groups, and their position is not much different now than it was earlier.

Obviously, judging by this table, the smaller independent producers are maturing their armagnacs for longer periods, on average, than either *négoçiants* or co-ops. This can only bode well for their future, and for the quality of what I have dubbed 'farmagnacs'. Armagnac, or the best of it anyway, looks like surviving into the 21st century. But the education process by BNIA, as well as various offshoots of SOPEXA (Food & Wine from France) must continue. There are still far too many markets where far too much armagnac is sent in cask. I would say this applies even to France's own interior market. Why, for instance should the *Cidrerie Montgommery* in Normandy 'produce' an armagnac? Why does it not stick to Calvados? The same goes for a round dozen Cognac houses, some Bordeaux (and even Burgundy!) merchants, and at least two in Alsace.

That last name is perhaps the best and safest pointer to the future. There is no bottling of Alsace wines or spirits outside its own *appellation controlée*; everything is matured and bottled locally. Maybe we shall see the same happening one day in Armagnac.

Domestic Trade

*D*uring the past few years, armagnac (the spirit) has begun to make some impact both in the UK and the USA. The professional organisation charged with promoting it (*Le Bureau National Interprofessionnel de l'Armagnac*, generally referred to as BNIA) has made great strides in getting it better known and more widely appreciated. A number of books, both in French and English, have also appeared. But all seemed to me to some extent unsatisfactory, in that they leave unanswered too many questions.

I might say unasked, rather than unanswered. This applies even to the most thorough and scholarly of such books: Henri Dufor's *L'Armagnac – Eau de Vie et Terroir* (Ed. Privat, Toulouse 1982). Monsieur Dufor, who regrettably died in 1987 while researching a second edition of his book, (on which he had already spent half a lifetime) has certainly done more than anyone else to dig up little-known facts and figures. Yet again and again, as I read his book I came across maddening hints which were left unexplored – and which therefore I decided to explore further.

This is particularly noticeable as regards the trade in armagnacs both in Europe and overseas, and more particularly in the UK and USA. Dufor tells us, for example, that the American trade was opened up during the War of Independence (1776–83) when imports of Scotch whiskies were blocked. But he tells us little else: which were the ports of entry, for example, who were the importers, much less the shippers. And – or so it seemed to me as I thought further about all this – was not New Orleans and the whole of Louisiana a French possession throughout the eighteenth century until 1803? Should one not look there rather than to Boston much later on? To go back in time even further: New York was Nieuw Amsterdam until 1664. We read a great deal about the entrepreneurial spirits of Dutch merchants in the

Vineyard in the Armagnac region. Not much changed over two centuries.

seventeenth century, but nothing specific about what they may have sent to the Dutch Antilles or that mainland American possession of theirs.

Gaps much closer to home are even more remarkable. Only one English name appears in the whole of Dufor's book: a certain Henry Thornton, Bordeaux *négoçiant*, who in 1647/8 shipped large quantities of *eaux-de-vie* (unspecified) – but to Middelburg in Holland, not to England! I will admit it is indeed difficult to trace references to the word 'armagnac' in English sources: the great *Oxford English Dictionary* illustrates no use of the word (as opposed to region, with capital A) before 1850. (We may note in passing that 'coniack' was known from 1687, when it is mentioned in an advertisement in the *London Gazette*). It would appear, on the face of it, that armagnac was classed until quite recent times, simply among other brandies. Indeed, it so figures in two very recent pocket guides by James Long and Nicholas Faith, both entitled *Cognac and Other Brandies*. Apart from which, we have only (in English), a paperback in Christie's Wine publications series,

Domaine de Maupas, Mauleon d'Armagnac.

translated from the French, which has its virtues but is necessarily limited in scope.

As I began to delve more deeply, I began to seek answers to those questions which even Monsieur Dufor never posed.

La Direction et les collaborateurs de l'Armagnac Sempé seront heureux de vous recevoir à Aignan ainsi que les membres de votre Club, pour leur présenter leurs produits à l'Armagnac et leur Cocktail "Coup de Foudre".

Vous visiterez nos caves et recevrez un cadeau en souvenir de votre visite commentée.

Nous organiserons votre trajet et votre repas si vous passez à Aignan entre 10 h. 30 et 12 h. 30.   Téléphone (62) 09.24.48

Foreign Trade

It has been suggested that armagnac began to be exported almost from its beginnings, i.e. during the fifteenth century. Through the kindness of Mr John Thorne of Dagenham, an antiquarian bookseller specialising in books on wine and spirits, I was apprised of a volume published in Paris during 1947 by Editions Ponsot (now defunct) which has the following passage by one W. K. Castleton (about whom I can find out nothing more):

> Armagnac as a liqueur knew a vogue both in England and Scotland as long ago as the middle of the 14th (*sic!*) century. Indeed it had not been distilled many years before it made a somewhat sensational appearance on the Glasgow market where it was taken for a new kind of wine instead of a potent liqueur – much to the consumer's first delight and subsequent regret! At the outset the production of Armagnac was rudimentary, but in a few years the Abbots of Condom were selling eaux de vie of incontestable *finesse* under that name.
>
> Within a comparatively short period the craze for armagnac had spread from Scotland down across the border and in the early part of the 15th century Glasgow was shipping linen, sheets, coal and herrings to Bordeaux and exchanging these commodities for salt, pepper, resin, plums and eaux-de-vie, among the latter some called Armagnac.

I do not know where Mr Castleton obtained his information at the time; I could certainly get no confirmation of it from Glasgow. In fact, the local reference library denied all knowledge of archives dating back so far. Mr Castleton was perhaps on firmer ground when he goes on to say:

APPELLATION ARMAGNAC CONTROLÉE

ARMAGNAC
Domaine de Tarrit

Roger LAGLEYZE
GAEC DE TARRIT
PROPRIÉTAIRE - RÉCOLTANT
TARRIT - CONDOM - GERS

70 cl.   40% vol.

> ... it may be recorded that the authentic documents surviving since 1616 show that the eaux-de-vie of Larressingle were utilised by many of the Benedictine Abbeys of both France and Spain, for the preparation of their elixirs, some of which have become, and still remain, world-famous.

Indeed, the spread of armagnac via monks and pilgrims in early days is highly likely – especially when we remember the medicinal origins of distilling, and the use of such distillations as 'cordials', i.e. restoratives. Indeed one of the most famous of all pilgrimages was and is that to Santiago de Compostela in the north-western corner of Spain. There are various routes, but the most common and easiest is from Vézelay through Limoges and Périgueux, crossing the river Garonne at Port Sainte-Marie and thence straight through the Armagnac region, from Nérac to Aire-sur-Adour.

Condom and Larressingle lay directly along this route, as did Eauze and Nogaro, while Vic-Fezensac, a little to the south, would have been a staging-post for those coming from Le Puy and through Cahors (an alternative route, crossing the Garonne at Moissac). Taking this alternative route, you would be passing through the Ténarèze rather than Bas-Armagnac. Still, it is all armagnac country, from Lectoure to Plaisance.

Conversely, few pilgrims would have crossed the Charentes, the two *départements* which today make up cognac country. The third pilgrim route to Compostela started in

Paris, passing through Orleans, Tours and Bordeaux. To Bordeaux, English pilgrims might well have sailed direct, either from London or Amsterdam, on one of the ships ploughing back and forth for the wine trade. They would then continue through the Landes and the Basque country.

So, to sum up: cordials based on distilled spirits were largely prepared by monks; and Benedictine monks from Condom to Saint-Sever were ideally placed to meet pilgrims' needs. Of course, major towns and villages were, for those travelling on foot, still too far apart for a day's journey and night's rest. This explains the many wayside chapels and abandoned hostels that can still be seen throughout the Gers along what used to be old pilgrim roads and are now mere tracks.

But I digress: we were talking of exports, not of the road to Compostela, about which there are several books that detail such sights. I daresay that by 1616 some armagnac had found its way to the Benedictine abbeys of Melrose and Pluscarden in Scotland. Whether they did so to similar abbeys in England before Henry VIII abolished the monasteries I would not care to say. Nor whether they came to Scotland via Glasgow or the Edinburgh port of Leith. And if they came from Bordeaux via Amsterdam rather than along some pilgrim road, I doubt if we are dealing with armagnac in any true sense.

I would say that this applies right up to the middle of the eighteenth century, when at last we read of some Cazaubon (Gers) *négoçiants*, and when shipping from Bayonne as well as

Bordeaux is documented. Even so, the traffic from Bayonne (of Dutch vessels, who throughout the seventeenth and eighteenth centuries dominated the French wine and spirit trade) was less than 5% of that from Bordeaux. And no French ship sailed from Bayonne to the French colony of Louisiana (more precisely to New Orleans) before 1750. Previous to this, all trade between France and Louisiana had emanated from Bordeaux, La Rochelle or Nantes. And though all such shipments included *eaux-de-vie* from 1726 onwards, again true armagnac would have been highly unlikely. Even in 1750 and departing from Bayonne, the cargo is still simply classed as *eaux-de-vie* and not further specified. Meanwhile, the cognac trade was already flourishing, and references to cognac – even to specific brands of this – occur quite often in shipping manifests or customs records.

French sources state that the American armagnac trade really took off during the War of Independence, when imports of Scotch whiskies were barred for patriotic reasons. Again, however, distances being what they are, not forgetting the relative isolation of the Armagnac region, Cognac would have benefited more. So we read, in old American newspapers of the time, of cognac, of Spanish brandies, of rum and arrack, but not of armagnac.

Who discovered it and, to whatever small extent, popularised it in the USA remains obscure. I daresay that if I had ten years to research this in newspaper files through American libraries, I could in the end trace it back to half a dozen enterprising importers in the same number of western USA seaboard cities, from Boston to Charleston. As I write

Columbian Centinel.

NO. 17, Vol. 45.]   BOSTON, (Massa.) SATURDAY,   APRIL 26, 1806.   [WHOLE NO. 2306.

The upper columns of the newspaper (Notices, Centinel News, Port of Boston—1806, National Legislature, Senate April 13, 1806, House of Representatives, Secret Journal) are printed in small type and largely illegible.

---

blue NANKINS, entitled

Spanish Dollars.   ap 26

n Fenno,

, *Has for sale,*
ooner *Sylph*, from *New*-
of 598 qtls. Merchant-
es and 18 barrel salmon,
r. 26.

Bryant,

f, *Has for*
ai ster Park, el.
apr. 26.

x Parker,

No 8, *Phillips' Buildings,*
beral credit,
Nankins, of a superior
back.   april 26

hard D. Harris,

posite *Old State-House.*
the *John Adams,* part of

MMER GOODS,

ities ; 6-4 Cambric do ;
Handkerchiefs, with par-
women's white, black and
i and twilled Grandarells ;
kins, 7-8, 4-4, 11-8, and 6-4,
ks ; 9 8 striped Cotton ;

killing of black striped satins, siletia ws, buntings,
embroidering Silks, &c ; 150 pieces Ravens
Duck ; 1 case Oil of Cinnamon ; 50 boxes white
and brown Havana Sugars ; few chests first quality Hyson Tea ; hhds Rum and Sugar ; pipes
Cognac Brandy ; few tons Pig Lead.

Also, landing from ship Hancock—100 chests Hy-
sonskin and Souchong Tea, of a very superior quality ; 32 boxes elegant China Ware.

French Brandy and Claret.

NOW landing, opposite No 60, *Long Wharf,*
and for sale, by JONATHAN DAVIS, No
2, said Wharf, the cargo of the schr *Mercator,* from
Bordeaux—being

150 pipes Armagnac Brandy; and 300 cases
Claret Wine, of superior quality.

If not sold at private sale, it will be sold at Ven-
due, at 11 o'clock, This Day.   april 26

Silk Hats.

JOHN FOX, No 60, *Cornhill,* has for sale, a few
cases men's fashionable Leghorn Silk Hats.
Also—fine 4-4 and 7 8 Irish Linens, Sheetings,
Cambrics, and Cambric Handkerchiefs.   ap 26

English Nails.

AN invoice of assorted English Nails, consisting
of 160 casks—for sale by S. & H. HIGGIN-
SON, No. 4, *Merchants-Row.*   april 23

Flax, Grass Seed, &c.

FOR SALE, at No. 60, Ann-street, a lot of
good clean Flax—Also, Clover and Herds'

---

scriber has been
trix to the last will and t

JOHN WOOI

late of *Machias,* in the
man, deceased, and
self that trust, by giving
All persons having dem
the said deceased, are
same ; and all persons in
are called upon to make

MEHITABI
' *Machias, April* 10, 180

WE the subscrib
pointed by the H
Judge of Probate for the
receive and examine the
tors to the estate of

JAMES

late of *Machias,* in said c
represented insolvent : I
months are allowed to sa
prove their claims ; and
service at the house of *Jo*
on the first Saturday of
from three till fix o'clock
JOSIAH HAR
MOSES HOV
PETER TALI
Machias, April 10, 18

Ten Dolla

RAN AWAY, from

Relfs Philadelphia Gazette,

AND DAILY ADVERTISER.

"Whatever measures have a tendency to dissolve the Union, or contribute to violate or lessen the Sovereign Authority, ought to be considered as hostile to the Liberty and Independence of America." WASHINGTON.

VOL. XXXIV.] WEDNESDAY, 11th JUNE, 1817. [No. 8850.

Philadelphia & Baltimore
LINE OF

Steam Boats and Stages.

By way of Wilmington & Elkton,
EVERY MONDAY, WEDNESDAY & FRIDAY.

THE Steam Boat SUPERIOR, capt. Milner, will leave the first wharf above Market-street, Philadelphia, at 3 o'clock in the after noon on the aforesaid days for *Baltimore*.

The Steam Boat NEW-JERSEY, capt. Rogers, will leave Light-street wharf, *Baltimore*, for *Philadelphia*, in the afternoon of the same days. These Boats are connected by a line of Stages, established on the *new Turnpike* between Wilmington and Elkton.

NB. The SUPERIOR, will leave *Philadelphia every day* for Wilmington, (Sundays excepted) at *three* in the afternoon, and Wilmington *every morning* for Philadelphia, at *seven o'clock*.

Passengers received and delivered at Chester and Marcus Hook. may 5—¶

Steam Boat Notice.
UNION LINE,
For Baltimore via New Castle & French Town.

The Delaware, W. Whilldin, master

For Bordeaux,
The regular trading copper bottomed
Ship Magnet,
R. Garwood, master;
She will sail with all possible dispatch. For freight or passage, having handsome accommodations, apply to the captain on board at Willing's wharf, or at the Counting house of
William Leedom,
june 7—¶ No. 78 s. F[illegible]-street

For Boston,
The regular trading sloop
Haymaker,
William Weeks, master;
Will be despatched immediately. For freight or passage, apply to the master on board, at the first wharf below Walnut str. or to
Perit & Cabot,
No. 123, south Front-street.
Who have for sale, landing from said sloop,—
N. E RUM, in hhds. june 2—¶

Ship Lancaster.
THE Consignees of Goods by this ship, are respectfully requested to send their permits on board at the subscribers wharf, as the ship is intended to be immediately returned
To Liverpool,
Having a considerable part of her cargo ready to go on board—some freight and passengers may still be accommodated.
Thos. P. Cope & Son.
For sale on board,—
50 tons Coal, 1800 bars Hammered Iron, 250 firkins Irish Butter, 5 casks Cutlery and 20 trunks, etc. Dry Goods may 7—¶

For Buenos Ayres.
The ship
George Washington,
James Yeardsley, master;
Will sail in about ten days. A few Goods will be taken on Freight. Apply to
Buck & Krambhaar.
May 5—¶

For Sale or Charter,
The fast sailing Pilot Boat
Schr Hebe.
Burthen 70 tons; lying at W[illegible]der's wharf, N L. is ready to receive a cargo. Apply to
Samuel B. Morris,
No. 6, South Wharves.
Who has landing and for sale,
28 bales Upland Cotton, and
43 hhds Green Copperas. april 29—¶

For Petersburgh---*direct*
The [illegible] trading
Sloop Phoebe,
Captain Skinner;
Having part of her freight engaged, she will sail with all possible dispatch. For the remainder or passage, apply on board at Lloyd's wharf 3d above the drawbridge, or to
Daniel C. Ellis,
No 50, South Wharves.
Who has for sale—
A few square bales Upland COTTON.
june 9—d3t

For Richmond--*direct*
The Regular trading
Schr. Molly.
Captain Somers;
Having two-thirds of her cargo on board, she will sail in the course of a few days. For freight of the remainder, apply on board, at Tunis and Way's wharf, first above the Drawbridge, or to
Daniel C Ellis,
june 9—d3t No 50, south wharves

For Baltimore,
The regular trading sloop
Young Man's Companion,
Capt. Adams;
Intended to sail in a few days.—For freight, apply at Hamilton's wharf, first above the drawbridge, or to
Daniel C. Ellis,
June 9—d3t No. 50, south wharves,

For Charleston, S. C.
The Packet
Ship Georgia Packet
Jared Bunce, Master;
Will sail on Thursday next. For freight or passage, having excellent accommodations, apply to the Captain on board, at Girard's wharf, or to
Samuel Brooks,
On said Wharf.
For sale as above—
88 bales prime Upland Cotton
[illegible] Rice june 7—d5t

For Georgetown, S. C.
The Brig
George Town Packet,
[illegible] Hewes, jr. master;
Will sail on the 14th inst. For freight or passage, having superior accommodations, apply to the master on board at Girard's wharf, or to
Allen & Taylor,
Who have for sale, received by said vessel,
[illegible] COTTON

For Liverpool,
The fine Philadelphia built and coppered
Ship Thalia.
Robert Morris, master;
Now lying at Girard's wharf, will sail on SUNDAY next, the 15th inst. weather permitting—has handsome accommodations for passengers. For passage only apply to the captain on board or to
Eyre & Massey,
Second Wharf below Chesnut st.
Who have for sale—
130 pipes fourth proof Armagnac Brandy of an excellent quality
100 casks Bordeaux Claret, 4 Iron Hoops on each, in fine order, and of superior quality,
100 cases old Medoc, vintage of 1811.
50 cases of choice of Chatteau Margeau, vintage of 1811
One Trunk India Mull Muslin,
Camphor,
Seine Twine,
Seersuckers, and
Dry English White Lead.
june 10—d6t

For St. Pierres, Mart. and St. Thomas,
The well known fast sailing
Sloop Morning Star,
Z Butler, master;
Having part of her cargo engaged. For freight of the remainder which will be taken on moderate terms, apply on board at Sims's wharf, or at the corner of Almond and Second-street, at capt. residence, or at No. 22, Chesnut-street.
NB A few passengers can be handsomely accommodated, having every convenience for the same. june 10—d4t

For Savannah. Geo.
The
Packet sloop Frolic,
Capt. Bateman;
Having part of her cargo engaged, will positively sail in one week. For freight or passage, apply on board at Hodge's wharf, or to
Bevan & Porter.
june 10—d3t No 22, south wharves.

For Freight or Charter.
To any part of the WEST-INDIES.
The substantial fast sailing copper bottomed British
Brig Hope,
Joseph Hall, Master,
Burthen about 2000 Barrels and ready to receive a cargo. Apply to
E Brown,

Economy.
Slater's Patent Steam Kitchen.
JUST received by the late arrivals, a further supply of SLATER'S highly approved Patent Steam Kitchen Range—particularly adapted for Steam Boats, Hotels, Public or Private Institutions, Boarding Houses, or Private Families, with apparatus complete, to cook for from 8 to 100 persons, and can be neatly fitted up in a small space, by a person acquainted with the principle. Price from 130 to $380 each—the terms of payment made easy to the purchaser.

Persons desirous of being satisfied of the *cleanliness, utility* and *actual savings* of meals and fuel, in the use of the above *Kitchen Range*, can be fairly convinced, by reference to one now fitted up, for inspection, and Certificates from the most respectable authorities, at
AY. SLATER & CO.
Agents to the Patentee, No. 28 Chesnut st.

The following, selected from a number of respectable testimonials of the great importance and saving of Slater's Steam Patent Kitchen Range, are submitted to the public:

Copy of Sir Thomas Plumer's Note.
The Vice Chancellor of England, authorised Mr Slater to say, that after 12 months experience of his Steam Apparatus, he can speak in the highest praise of it, as fully answering every object intended, especially the cleanliness of it, and great saving of fuel. The Vice Chancellor being so much pleased with the one fitted up in his town in use, has since had another erected at his country seat, and will at any time be most happy to have it shewn to any one Mr Slater should wish may see it, and will explain the great and certain advantages resulting from so useful and clever an invention.
Upper Guilford street, No. 71
5th December, 1815.

Extract from the letter of Capt. Maling R. N. H. M. ship Mulgrave, dated 28th July 181[illegible]
With regard to the *Cooking* Apparatus, [illegible] happy to acquaint you that it answered *perfectly*, and you have my authority to use of my name and to declare, that it not cooked *every thing* used at my table, but for the wardroom, and even for the crew; it never was out of order, and was used, and found particularly useful in gales of wind. Had the war lasted, I am confident they would have become general in the navy, for no one saw the one I had without approving of it, among others, I may mention Admirals Sir B. Hallowell, Sir [illegible], Sir Geo Burlton, &c. and several captains.

PS. I particularly recommend your Cooking Apparatus for East and West Indiamen, & large merchant ships, both as an accommodation and saving of fuel. Yours, etc
[Signed] CAPTAIN MALING.
June 7—stuth6t

Indigo.

---

t Lever Watches.
[e]legant assortment of Gold [WAT]CHES, with wreath cases [w]orkmanship, wholesale &

F. Reid,
No. 150, Market-street.

[HI]DES.
Prime Buenos Ayres Ox
. Apply to
Richard Willing,
No. 21, Penn-street.

[D]elaware Insurance [of] Philadelphia,
June 2d, 1817.
[Th]e Company, have this day [a dividen]d of five per centum, or [per] share of the company's [to th]e stockholders, or their [a]t any time after the 12th [SA]MUEL KEITH, Pres't.

[Ge]ntleman
[o]f making a tour through [Sta]tes previously to settling [serv]ices to any merchants to [thei]r accounts. He will go [a]s west of Pennsylvania,

100 hhds Muscovado Sugars
100 boxes brown Havanna
100,000 lbs coffee in bbls & bags
100 hhds Sweet Molasses
} Entitled to drawback
May 30—fmw6t

Black Ostrich Feathers,

A Small BOX——Received per ship Magnet, just arrived from Bordeaux, and for sale by
J. J. Borie, jr,
June 9—d3t No 182, Market st.

JUST ARRIVED

IN Ship Thalia, Robert Morris, master from Bordeaux :—
130 pipes of fine Armagnac 4th proof Brandy
100 casks of superiour quality Claret
100 cases Old Medoc, vintage 1811.
50 cases fine old Claret, growth of Chalteau Margeau, vintage of 1811.
For sale by
Eyre & Massey,
Second Wharf below Chesnut st
Who have also for sale—
India Mull Muslins, very fine,
Seersuckers
Seine Twine,
Camphor, and
English White Lead June 4—d6t

Cotton.

FIFTY Bales prime Georgia Upland Cotton. For sale at

[...]years themselves in the [...] assure the public, that [...] in this line shall have d[...] every respect, which m[...] pers. as the captains are [...] Goods and Packages [...] Stationers, Booksellers, [...] to this line from any par[...] shall be put on board [...] transported by land if r[...] ter season, free of exper[...] incurred previous to the [...] be advanced, receivabl[e] freight when the goods [...] delphia or New-York.

At New-York, apply t[o] of Dispatch Line of Re[...] delphia, 30 Old Slip.

At Philadelphia, apply [...] gent at the Dispatch [...] Packets to New-York, u[...] Counting Room, Chesnut [...]

By inquiry at the ab[...] may always be had of t[...] these vessels.

P GRIM, respectfull[y] that he will transact busi[ness un]der the old firm of David [...]ly on his own account, an[...]
june 10—d1m

Upland C[otton]

NINETEEN bales Up[land ... supe]rior quality, just la[nded]

this, I have found only two clues. The first is an advertisement for '130 pipes of Armagnac brandy' in the *Columbian Centinel* (Boston) of 26 April 1806; the second takes us on to 1817, when the firm of Eyre and Massey offer 130 pipes of 'fourth proof Armagnac Brandy of an excellent quality' for sale in *Relph's Philadelphia Gazette* of 11 June that year.

Now it so happens that quite a bit is known about the merchant house of Eyre and Massey in Philadelphia. It flourished from around 1780–1860, had a high reputation, and a fleet of ships which traded throughout the world, including – as mentioned specifically in one source – the port of Bayonne. We may take it, therefore, that Eyre & Massey knew exactly what they were offering – especially since the same advertisement also mentions '50 cases of choice Chatteau Margeau, vintage of 1811'. And the fact that the armagnac is advertised as 'fourth proof', that is the highest rather than lowest permitted alcoholic strength, also shows that Eyre & Massey had a discriminating clientele. The best armagnac is always sold at 'barrel proof', not reduced with distilled water.

Turning to England, I could find no remotely similar advertisement, even ten years later, when the popular magazine *John Bull* carried regular announcements of goods landed in the Port of London. I find cognac – even Cognac Otard, listed at a premium price – and all manner of other spirits and brandies, including 'Cette' (i.e. the port of Sète in the Languedoc, where cheap and nasty wines were turned into at least tolerable distilled spirits).

I fear we must conclude that the English wine trade was too wedded to cognac, and of course to port, to make the effort of introducing yet another brandy. Cognac, thus particularised by name, appears in a *London Gazette* advertisement as early as 1687; armagnac I know not when. Most likely the great Oxford dictionary is correct in stating that it does not appear here (as a word, not a geographical region) before 1850, and that George Saintsbury in 1920 (*Notes on a Cellar Book*) was the first to appreciate its qualities. We are, after all, a pretty conservative race. And the phylloxera, from the 1870s onwards, even drove out the Englishman's brandy and soda in favour of whisky and soda – at any rate for a number of years.

So it is not perhaps surprising to find an extraordinary ignorance regarding armagnac as late as 1909 expressed before the Royal Commission on Whiskies and other Potable Spirit by Mr Arthur Southard, a leading London wine merchant of that time. Here is part of the dialogue, verbatim, between him and the Commission's chairman, while giving evidence:

17501. Will you tell us something about the Algerian brandies? – The Algerian brandies are grown from the same vine that grows the best French brandy in Cognac, a vine called Folle Blanche, which yields a very large quantity of very delicate and pure brandy, and those brandies in my mind are the nearest approach to anything I have seen to the brandies of Cognac. They are extremely good, very pure, if anything a little too delicate for the public-house trade.

17502. Is there much trade with the Algerian brandies in this country? – Yes, some of our largest houses buy them now and find them extremely useful.

17503. How would they compare in quality with the Cognac brandy? – They compare so well that in one of my recent circulars I had to mention that the quality of the 1908 brandy that had just been made approached very nearly to the very best Cognac that

you get from the Charente. They are extremely good.

17504. And as to price? – Half.

17505. Is the trade increasing? – The Algerian colonies produce an enormous quantity of wine. There are some firms in Algeria that produce 40,000 to 50,000 hogsheads in one season. Brandy, if I know anything at all about it, is the result of the overproducing of new wine which had to be burnt down and converted into brandy for the sake of reducing the bulk, and in Algeria at the present moment they have such a quantity of wine, and such beautiful wine too that they are obliged to distil some of the wine so as to accommodate the stock to the storage that they may give to it. They have to make wine to keep as wine. It decomposes and deteriorates with the heat of the summer, and under those circumstances they found that turning it into brandy was the best means of preserving it.

17506. Now as to the third class of brandy, the Armagnac brandy? – The Armagnac brandies are brandies that have been known for centuries. They are grown all in the South of France in the neighbourhood of Béziers. That is the centre of the Armagnac trade, and they have a large output in France, but they do not take in this country. They are rather soft, they have no nerve and no grip, and they are not popular.

17507. Are they cheaper or not? – Oh, no. They rank a little cheaper than the Cognac brandy but not much.

17508. Is there much trade in them? – We cannot make it, we have tried very hard. I have some splendid houses to back us with the stuff, but we cannot get the British merchant to take them up. There is not sufficient difference between their price and the quality to induce the merchant who wants the best to go away from the best.

17509. Excuse me putting a simile to you, but, supposing you were treating this matter as a matter of racehorses, how should you place these three brandies 1st, 2nd and 3rd? – Undoubtedly Algerian first, second Armagnac, and third Egyptian.

No wonder that Food and Wine from France, in a very recent publicity campaign, had to refer to Armagnac as 'France's best kept Secret'. At least we may hope that no English wine merchant today thinks that Béziers lies anywhere near Gascony. Nor do we hear much of the excellence of Algerian brandies these days (in fact, my enquiries as to whether they were still sold in the UK led to another dead end).

Even today, armagnac sales abroad are only about 10% of cognac sales overall – and in England very much less. The biggest increase and rather sudden upsurge in sales has been in the USA. Darroze, the famous restaurateur of Villeneuve de Marsan and *négociant* in armagnacs at Roquefort (Landes) has his own agent/distributor there; and even on a much smaller scale, astute Americans are combing the Gascony countryside and laying claim to much of the best produce of small producers who would never dream of publicising what little they have to sell. 40% of all armagnac never leaves the region, and 80% of the remainder stays in France, with direct sales to top hotels, restaurants and private customers. It was something of an eye-opener to stumble across the *Domaine de Maupas* (not nearly as grand as it sounds, just a large farm really, surrounded by vineyards) and find attached to a bottle of its 1964 vintage a typed slip, reading: 'Imported to the United States by the Tilland Family Wine Co., Denver, Colorado'. That's a good 3,000 miles from New York even, never mind the 2,000 miles across the Atlantic; yet I have still to track down the *Domaine de Maupas* much nearer home.

I am afraid that the branded goods market is much to blame for the state of affairs in England. Yet I cannot really blame Janneau for riding high on the back of Martell; I say 'the best of luck to it' on supermarket shelves – and now, since Seagram have taken over Martell, more of it at Oddbins too. But this is not, as I have stressed before but cannot stress too much, what real armagnac is all about. At its best, it remains a cottage industry, with all the individuality which this implies, not some bland blend. It is for those who (in wine terms) can distinguish an estate in Pomerol from one a few miles away in St Emilion – and both from a Fronsac; and who can appreciate each for its own qualities, without hankering after the other. When, I wonder, will more of our wine merchants wake up to this fact?

Tasting

*T*here is, first and foremost, one crucial difference between the tasting of wines and spirits. The spitoon has no place in the latter. Either you simply sniff or you drink it down; you certainly don't spit it out – that would be sacrilege almost!

Professionals go in for sniffing, or for swilling just a few drops of armagnac round their mouth, on the tongue, where most of it then evaporates before they actually down what remains. By professionals I mean those whose business it is to judge and possibly blend from various producers and regions, and of different ages. Much the same, of course, applies to cognacs and whiskies, where a constant 'house style' year in year out is deemed of primary importance.

I cannot begin to talk even half intelligently (or intelligibly) about such skills. In any case, even before tasting, your expert will hold the glass up to judge the liquid's colour. Here, my credulity becomes somewhat strained, as we all know what can be done with a little caramel or other agent. The custom of adding such is, however, not nearly as widespread in the Armagnac region as elsewhere; the smaller and better producers will have no truck with it. A deep amber colour from a small *domaine* specialising in stated age or vintage armagnacs is usually the result of long ageing in the traditional dark oak barrels.

The tasting chart, therefore, which I present opposite, is something far beyond my ken – and probably that of most amateur tasters. I would advise cutting down the list of qualities to be judged to about six or seven – the more so because you need to swallow and should not spit out. What the French call *le retour* means simply the pleasant 'return' of the spirit after you have ingested it; the well-being you feel in the pit of your stomach which makes for a good after-dinner drink (which is, after all, why they are called *digestifs*).

FICHE DE DEGUSTATION D'ARMAGNAC

EXAMEN VISUEL

ASPECT

- brillant ☑
- limpide ☑
- terne ☐

PRESENCE DE PARTICULES

- OUI ☐
- NON ☐

COULEUR

- Jaune ☑
- Orange ☑
- Acajou ☐
- Vert pombé ☐

INTENSITE

- Clair ☑
- Moyen ☐
- Foncé ☐

APPRECIATION VISUELLE

- Insuffisant ☐
- Médiocre ☐
- Moyen ☐
- Bon ☑
- Excellent ☑

IMPRESSION GENERALE

	OUI	NON
- Légère Maigre	☐	☐
- Riche Longue	☑	☐
- Equilibrée	☐	☐
- Jeune	☐	☐
- Boisée	☐	☐

EXAMEN OLFACTIF
(nez + voie rétro Nasale)

INTENSITE

faible	moyen	fort
☐	☐	☑

ELEMENTS DE QUALITE

	OUI	NON
Odeur florale	☐	☐
Odeur fruité	☐	☐
Odeur de Pruneau	☐	☐
Odeur de Vanille	☐	☐
Odeur de bois	☐	☐
Odeur de Rancio	☐	☐

Autres odeurs agréables
. . . .
. . . .
. . . .

ELEMENTS DE DEFAUTS

Acescence	☐	☐
Piquant	☐	☐
Odeur d'alambic	☐	☐
Mauvais bois	☐	☐

Autres odeurs désagréables
. . . .
. . . .
. . . .

APPRECIATION OLFACTIVE

- Insuffisant ☐
- Médiocre ☐
- Moyen ☐
- Bon ☐
- Excellent ☐

. . . .

EXAMEN GUSTATIF

	faible	moyen	fort
Amplitude	☐	☐	☐
Rondeur	☐	☐	☑
Longueur	☐	☐	☐

	OUI	NON
Sécheresse	☐	☐
Astringence	☐	☐
Brulant	☐	☐
Sucré	☐	☐
Boisé	☐	☐

Autres éléments du goût
. . . .
. . . .

APPRECIATION GUSTATIVE

- Insuffisant ☐
- Médiocre ☐
- Moyen ☐
- Bon ☐
- Excellent ☐

COTATION

- Parfait	:	19–20
- Très bien	:	16–18
- Bien	:	12–15
- Moyen	:	10–12
- Passable	:	5–9
- Mauvais	:	1–5

(entourer la note choisie)

I have marked the qualities to look out for, with seven crosses on the chart. With this caution, moreover: any seven tasters would probably disagree about any seven given armagnacs! The best armagnac for you is the one you like best; trust your guts. There are now almost 100 to choose from in England alone, and many times more in the region itself.

My own tastes, as I have already hinted, veer towards the heavier, rounder, fuller styles of armagnac – what I have called 'farmagnacs', as produced by traditional small stills and matured without any reduction by means of distilled water. Such armagnacs are perhaps an acquired taste, as are the older style burgundies; the fashion today is for something lighter and more flowery. Someone brought up on austere fine clarets and Delamain Pale and Dry cognac might even find them nauseatingly rich. I have tried some *Domaine de Juglaron* (one of my favourites from near Eauze) on friends and seen them pull odd faces. Such people should stick to a VSOP blend, among which there are plenty to choose now, in high street off-licences like Oddbins. They themselves recommend their *Larressingle*; I prefer the single-estate *Domaine de Pléchat* (10-year-old), and not only because it is £1 cheaper. It seems to me a more 'rounded' spirit, with altogether more character.

There was talk, some months ago, of Oddbins bringing out a range of miniatures, boxed as ten or even twelve; unfortunately, I have heard no more of this. They should do so, and the sooner the better, for armagnac tastings are few and far between. (And to buy twelve whole bottles, just to decide which suits your palate best, is an expensive game.) As frequently hinted, there is no substitute for a visit to Armagnac; hence this book and its maps.

Gastronomic Delights of Gascony

*I*t is not difficult to imagine the dashing Gascon, fiercely independent and contemptuous of authority, until you consider his diet. After that you begin to think that he must do most of his dashing in the morning, because if you have ever lunched on *côtes de porc à la Gasconne* you will know that the rest of the day should be spent on contemplative, rather than physical, pursuits.

The morning, therefore, is the time for hunting the game that thrives in the woods of western Gascony, and for catching the pike, shad, eels and lampreys that inhabit the lagoons. Apart from traditional game such as partridge, woodcock, quail and hare, the Gascons hunt ortolans (a member of the bunting family), quail, wild dove and thrush (*grives*). Many of the sauces in which these delicious birds take their final rest contain quantities of armagnac to enhance the meat bouillon. There is a wonderful dish, *bec-fins à la Landaise*, which both delights and confuses those who are not in the know. A *bec-fin* is a colloquial word for a gourmet, but Gascons enjoy perpetuating the myth that it is an appetising little bird which you wrap in a slice of bacon and a grape leaf. Then three are put on a skewer and cooked in fat from *foie gras*. The sauce, made from meat bouillon with a dash or three of armagnac is augmented with grape seeds. To eat it, you simply hold the bird by the beak and, as you begin to taste and smell the delicious meat and sauce, you will have the greatest difficulty in restraining yourself from popping it all in at once.

When at last you can speak again you will ask what sort of bird it is that can give such pleasure. The Gascon will smile and tell you that it is a *bec-fin*. But ask him to show you one with its feathers on and he will be strangely reticent.

If that sounds altogether too rich for you, then try one of the famous Gascon pigeon pasties, full of meat, diced vegetables

UN MENU GASCON

par Joseph PESQUIDOUX

and garlic, all cooked in goose-fat and covered in a substantial width of pastry.

Gascons, as you will have realised, enjoy being self sufficient. Most farms will be crammed full of preserved foods against the rainy day when the game birds don't fly and the fish don't bite. But what preserved food! Do you see all those geese? They are the basis, the staple commodity and the source of goose fat, *foie gras* and the preserved goose that emerges from a steaming casserole alongside the diced potatoes, onions and Bayonne ham which, like all Landes ham, is cured raw.

Take some of that ham, dice it, chop some onions, mix the ham and onion, brown them together in goose fat, then beat them in with eggs, garlic and parsley and cook them fast into an *omelette à la Gascon*. Oh yes! It must be cooked in goose fat.

It is the goose fat that provides the succulence for the *côtes de porc* that we mentioned earlier. Gascons regard cooking in butter as very much second best. In fact the Greeks regarded goose fat as having aphrodisiac properties. When you have tasted the pork chops, marinated, fried in the fat, and cooked in sauce made from bouillon and wine – you may agree with them.

Or you may think that most of the food described so far is farmers' food, rather than restaurant food. Well so it is, and none the worse for that, although there is not a restaurant in the world which would not be proud to serve *bec-fins*. But the real heart of Gascon gastronomy is to be found in Armagnac itself. This is the region which gave birth to *estouffat* (or *estouffade*), one of the bases of all covered pot cooking. So when we talk of pork or beef *estouffat*, although we tend to mean pork or beef cooked in any covered pot, we would be more correct to mean meat cooked in the original *estouffat*,

made from boiling down veal, lean beef, marrow bones, pork fat, ham, carrots, potatoes, onions, garlic and herbs. The resulting miraculous liquid imparts its magical properties to creations such as Gascon shoulder of lamb, stuffed with hashed ham, onions, garlic, eggs and bread soaked in bouillon, braised with vegetables and herbs.

The Établissement Ryste at Larressingle, producers of both armagnac and foie gras.

Some of the other masterpieces you can sample in the region are roast capon *à l'Artagnan*, a dashing dish with more than a dash of armagnac added; *poule en compote*, stewed in the rich juices we have described, and the noted local method of cooking cabbage in cream – it is delicious.

The ubiquitous goose fat is provided by the ubiquitous goose, which in its turn is fed (or perhaps we should say stuffed full of) the abundant maize. In passing, we might risk offending our Gascon hosts by asking whether any food is so delicious that it justifies the cruelty involved in cramming so much down the throat of the bird (often using a funnel) so that its liver distends, all for the sake of the much prized *foie gras*.

The sweet corn is also a feature of the human diet. It is never eaten on the cob in Gascony and more often forms the basis of dishes such as *millas* and *escauton* – a corn meal mash cooked in . . . you've guessed . . . goose fat.

Getting There

*I*t is, admittedly, neither quick nor cheap to reach our Elysian goal, and probably the main reason why Gascony (and consequently Armagnac) remain relatively little known by English holiday-makers. The advantage is, of course, that you will not be lost among a crowd of other tourists (as, for instance, in the Dordogne); if you go out of season, yours will probably be the only English voice around! Again, of course, this has its disadvantages if you speak no French.

But to the point: there are three main approaches: via Bordeaux, via Toulouse, or via Paris and Périgueux, continuing through the Dordogne to Villeneuve-sur-Lot where the road divides to take you either via Agen to Auch, the capital of Gers *département*, or along the D118 via Port-Ste-Marie to Lavardac.

If you dislike long road journeys, the air/car-rental arrangements available (both BA and Air France offer them) from Toulouse or Bordeaux are certainly convenient. I must stress that a car is absolutely essential for exploring the region (unless, of course, you are young and fit enough to brave all weather cycling, motorised or otherwise). Rail communications are practically non-existent within the Gers, except along the periphery and a sort of spur from Toulouse to Auch.

If you like neither long car journeys nor air travel, I would suggest rail as far as Agen. You will have to spend a night in Paris, which is no great hardship. I find French Rail superb, very reliable and relatively cheap, especially if you take advantage of their *France Vacances* pass, allowing unlimited travel over the entire network subject to certain conditions. Again, there are special rates for rail/car-rental combined.

The question as to which approach is best depends on what you want to see. Gascony is ideal for leisurely travel, not for

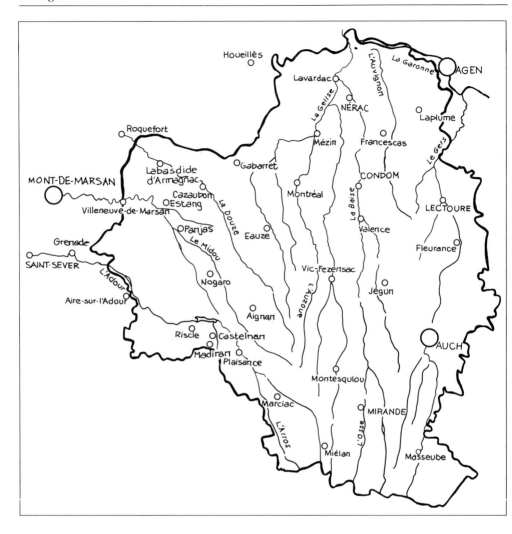

6 Musée du Vigneron XVII° S.
5   Domaine DURROUX
4   LUFLADE – MOUREOU
4   Domaine DULHOSTE
3   Domaine LUSSON

CAZAUBON 7

Signpost near Mauléon d'Armagnac. The Musée du Vigneron is part of Château Garreau.

tight-scheduled rushing-around; you need two or even three trips to see and appreciate it all. If your main concern is to visit some of the best properties in the *'Grand-Bas'*, then by all means take the autoroute from Bordeaux, and leaving it at Langon for Bazas and Roquefort. If I now advise you to hurry through Roquefort (not quite within the Bas-Armagnac area, anyway), it is because you might easily spend a small fortune at the establishment of Monsieur Francis Darroze. You would be better advised to continue in a south-easterly direction as far as Cazaubon, where demi-pension at Mme Bonnet's *Hôtel du Centre* (with liberal wine included) will cost you less than one of Monsieur Darroze's bottles. You will also – as the itineraries which follow will show – be at the centre of some of the best armagnac properties.

Toulouse makes sense if you wish to be more adventurous – and if you like to explore churches, abbeys and museums as well as simply armagnac. In Toulouse itself, I would suggest a visit for lunch to Monsieur Christian Lacoste rather than to yet another (expensive!) Darroze. He will tell you about his home town, Fleurance, and the *Distillerie Carrère* there. You could then make straight for Auch or make a detour via such delightful villages as Cologne and/or Mauvezin, not forgetting the already mentioned Saint-Clar. You will probably decide that the armagnacs on sale (at producer's prices!) in Monsieur Denis Vidal's charming boutique justify a week's stay in or around that village, not just a day. Wines and other delicacies are there in profusion, too. Besides, if you were at Auch, Monsieur Daguin of the famous *Hôtel de France* may already have alerted you to the fact that certain Ténarèze and even Haut-Armagnac spirits are worth trying. So I would be surprised if you ventured further than the river Baïse on any such trip; there is enough to see, let alone digest, in a fortnight.

If you come from the north, you are still in the Lot-et-Garonne *département* as you arrive at Lavardac. It is perhaps the best starting-point to get the best of all possible worlds. The prestigious house of Castarède is just off the road from the charming *Chaumière d'Albret*. You are also just a few kilometres from *Château Pierron*, and a dozen other properties shown on our maps. Venturing east, you are in the Pays d'Agenais where you will find yet other distillations: fruit brandies of great delicacy. Although these do not, strictly speaking, fall within my brief, I must at least mention the extraordinary *Distillerie Saint Gayrand* at Moncaut. Apart from a full range of *eaux de vie blanches* they also produce the only *eau-de-vie de muscat* known to me (the grape chiefly known for the fine sweet wines it makes in the Gaillac region).

You could, I suppose, sidestep all such temptations and make straight for Condom or Eauze: centres of the armagnac region rather than on its periphery. But I think you would be missing out on much that is worthwhile and enjoyable.

Three More Approaches

*I*f you are prepared to contemplate a rather longer and more expensive air journey than to Bordeaux or Toulouse, there are three alternatives: flights to Biarritz, direct from London, to Pau, or to Tarbes in the Pyrenees, via Paris. Each of these has something to be said for it, especially if you have say three weeks' leisure and would like to combine a visit to Armagnac with a mountain or seaside holiday.

To take Biarritz first, as it is easiest if starting from England: its airport is halfway between that town and Bayonne (not more than 5 km from each); and Bayonne has strong Armagnac links anyway. It is the headquarters of Izarra, that armagnac-based liqueur rated second only to Chartreuse. Bayonne was, of course, also the principal port for shipping armagnacs (brought down from the market of Saint-Sever along the Adour) for over two centuries. Finally, and by no means of least interest to anyone from England, Bayonne was captured by Wellington upon his return from the Peninsular War early in 1814; and the Iron Duke thence made his way across some of the best armagnac country to Toulouse. So you can follow in his footsteps, via Orthez and Aire-sur-Adour, or go further north via Dax and Roquefort into the heart of the Bas-Armagnac.

Pau is surely the nearest airport of all for the south-western part of Armagnac: what is known as the *Basse-Rivière* (Adour) between Riscle and Aire. Here, you have the advantage of the Jurançon vineyards almost at the gates of Pau to the south-west of the town and, to the north-east, the vineyards of Madiran before reaching the *Basse-Rivière* (maybe even below Riscle, at Plaisance). The area of Armagnac you can now explore holds much of interest (it is near the point where Bas-Haut and Ténarèze meet). Pau and its *château* (where Henry IV, *le Vert Galant*, was born and baptised) should not be

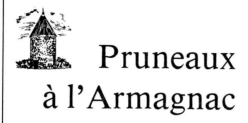

Pruneaux
à l'Armagnac

Domaine de Tarrit
GAEC de Tarrit

1ℓ

Roger LAGLEYZE
PROPRIÉTAIRE - RECOLTANT
TARRIT - CONDOM - GERS

20°

missed; nor the small town of Morlaas, one-time capital of Béarn, the mint of which gave the name to that coin, the *morlan*, of which we shall hear more anon.

Finally, Tarbes. This lies not more than 20 km from the most southerly point of the Gers *département*; and though this may not be an obvious starting-point for armagnac (the spirit), the countryside here is at its most beautiful, and halfway between Miélan and Montesquiou you will pass (or not pass, I hope) the *Château de Marignan*, which will prove to you just how good even an Haut-Armagnac can be, if properly tended and matured. (I forgot to mention that the airport of Tarbes in fact lies halfway between Tarbes and Lourdes, the latter a magnet for pilgrims.)

In short, there is something to be said for almost every way of access. Come by car from the north, cross the river at Port Ste-Marie, and you can see the glassworks at Vianne shortly before reaching Lavardac. Cross the river at Agen somewhat to the east and you pass through some of the best fruit-growing country in France, and will pass also through villages where fruits in armagnac or *prune d'ente* (*eau de vie* made of plums) are sold. One route from Bordeaux has already been described; you can, if you like, follow the Garonne further upstream as far as Marmande, where there are excellent wines, too. And from Toulouse, apart from the route north-west through the Lomagne, you can motor straight to Auch if you prefer. But everywhere you will find places begging you to idle for an hour or a day even. And though you may not be in armagnac country proper, you will certainly be offered some, long before you reach the river Baïse.

Napoleon greeted by local people near Bayonne in 1808.

Stylish, and slightly more modern, vehicles in which to explore.

The Bas-Armagnac

*T*he least hilly and the most sandy of the three regions, the Bas-Armagnac is, because of its soil and subsoil, the one that consistently yields the best spirit. In other words, the prefix *bas* (meaning low) refers purely to the lie of the land, not to what is produced there. It has as many hectares under vine (around 5,000) as does the Ténarèze, but much more of the produce is *domaine*-bottled here. Generally speaking, the further west you go, the better the quality. The very best area of all is concentrated within the Landes *département*, west of Cazaubon towards Labastide d'Armagnac, from which one may draw a line roughly southwest (towards Aire-sur Adour). Being roughly triangular in shape the locals often refer to it as 'the golden triangle'. They also give it the unofficial appelation *'le Grand-Bas'*.

Twenty-five years ago, Messrs Jaquelin and Poulain in their *Vines and Vineyards of France* allowed only three communes the right to this name: the districts surrounding Castex, Monclar and Monlezun. Today, of the 60 communes in the Gers and 24 in the Landes it would be fair to say that about one-third lay claim to it, of which most are in the Landes. Much of the quality is due to careful replanting. During the 1960s, a disease known locally as *flavascence dorée* swept through the vineyards and led to a great deal of replanting. Stocks were at one time so much reduced as to represent only two years' sales (as opposed to an average of six). It was not until the 1970s, and by dint of rigorous rationing of sales, that some sort of equilibrium was restored.

One can easily understand, therefore, that many small growers faced ruin. Even though an armagnac made from the *folle blanche* or from the *Baco 22A* (the most favoured grapes in this region) tends to be softer and to mature more rapidly than a Ténarèze, an owner would want to wait at least seven and

The Château de Maniban, at Mauléon d'Armagnac.

138

preferably ten years before offering his armagnac for sale. It is here that we must salute Francis Darroze of Roquefort and the *Frères Fatima* of Auxil, both in the Landes.

The *Restaurant Darroze* at Villeneuve de Marsan has long been celebrated: two stars in Michelin even 30 years ago under Jean Darroze. It has meanwhile grown into a fine hotel, second only perhaps to Guérard's world-famous *Les Prés d'Eugénie*. It is to Francis Darroze's great credit that he has saved many of the finest small properties from almost certain extinction, investing heavily in their inherent quality. That is to say, he has built an ideal *chai* on two levels, with separate humidity controls for each. He buys the distilled spirit from the growers (with distillation always by means of the *alambic armagnacais* at around 53° vol; he finances the casks and the years of ageing. The *domaine* of origin, together with dates of both distillation and of bottling, are always stated on his bottles. Of course, he also offers these same armagnacs in his restaurant, the profits from which make the whole operation viable.

To the best of my knowledge, none of the dozen and a half or so different armagnacs sold by Darroze are available in England; but he has a USA agent. I have, however, seen the *Frères Fatima* on sale at Fortnum's. This extraordinary religious brotherhood also operates two high-class restaurants, at Dax and Magescq; moreover, it imports rare malt whiskies as another profitable sideline. Their selection is rather smaller and probably put together more on an ad hoc basis; some of the vintages they offer, always in small parcels only, go back to pre-war days.

The church at Salles d'Armagnac, opposite the château.

For our purposes, i.e. visiting and sampling at the property, I have omitted all mention of such Bas-Armagnacs: I merely show you both Roquefort and Auxil on the general map. The latter, indeed, lies well outside the region, nearer the coast towards Bayonne.

Moving from the Ténarèze into the Bas-Armagnac, our own first call must be at Eauze. In fact, this small market town, today the administrative headquarters (i.e. seat of BNIA), was until 1909 deemed part of the Ténarèze. Today, as our first itinerary shows, it is surrounded by some excellent properties:

I liked the *Hôtel Henri IV*, by the church right in the centre of Eauze, even though the service was a bit slapdash and the

bedroom bare of pictures. You certainly could not better the 45 francs evening menu, which might include delicacies like wild boar, generous *hors d'oeuvres* of fish or *charcuterie*, soup for starters, cheese and fruit to finish. The bed was comfortable, the bathwater hot. With a good breakfast (fresh chunks of butter and homemade jam) it cost (including all drinks) less than 200 francs demi-pension in March 1988. The drinks would include a half-litre of wine at dinner, apéritif before and armagnac to follow. The hotel's house armagnac is a ten-year-old from the *Domaine de Juglaron* some 3 km out of town.

Where next? Eauze is very much of a hub. You could go north-west to Cazaubon, south-west to Nogaro, south-east to Lannepax or due west to Estang. Each has a pleasant if modest hotel at which to stay, none in *Michelin* or the *Logis de France* guide. But you would not be slumming it at any of them – viz

the *Hotel du Commerce* at Estang, *Hotel Bonnet* (Place de la Mairie) at Cazaubon and the *Hostellerie Gasconne* at Lannepax. Of these, I stayed with Madame Bonnet and had a Sunday lunch at Lannepax. The *Hostellerie Gasconne* lies at the corner of the village square and has a pleasant shaded garden. Again, the house armagnac was purely local, 4 km from the village: the *Domaine Gaston*, run by Max Dauriac. Lighter and somewhat younger than Juglaron at Eauze, but at under £10 per bottle a gift, I think. I have not bothered to map this, as you simply follow the D626 out of Lannepax for a couple of hundred yards or so, where you will see Gaston clearly signposted to your left (at St Roch).

Eauze at the turn of the century.

Follow the D626 further and you arrive within less than ten minutes at Vic Fezensac. This is a small excursion back into the Ténarèze, but worth it for the extraordinary Monsieur Marcel Trépout at his *Château Notre Dame*. He has been in the business for over 60 years as a blender and bottler, who watches carefully over each cask (chosen, of course, by himself alone). A very few of his bottles, like those of Laberdolive, find their way to England, though not into shops, only to the top end of the restaurant trade. A delicious *liqueur à l'orange*, based on armagnac and at full 40° vol, is one of his specialities and well worth 125 francs (1988 price). Marcel Trépout being another one-man band, is not always available; if he is, do not fail to ask to see (and sample) what he has to offer. You can also buy his products at a large wines/spirits shop as you enter Vic Fezensac, just before you turn into the main road for the centre of town.

As we move west, the further west we move, the more villages entitled to Bas-Armagnac appellation do we find. It is perhaps worth mentioning that in the Landes *département*, there are no co-operative cellars at all (as against six in the Gers), all producers in these 24 villages bottling their own or being within the net of Auxil or Darroze. There is also a *Syndicat des Producteurs* for the Landes armagnac growers quite separate from Eauze BNIA headquarters, and affiliated to the Landes *Chambre d'Agriculture* in Mont-de-Marsan.

The only notable exception to this rule is the *Compagnie Viticole des Grands Armagnacs* (SICA Gerland, part of the Camus Cognac group) headquartered at Vileneuve-de-Marsan. They produce numerous brands, and I hasten to add that all are distilled either at Villeneuve or at Labastide

Larry Hagman's favourite property.

BAS ARMAGNAC

APPELLATION BAS:ARMAGNAC CONTROLEE

CHATEAU de LASSALLE

Baronne H .de Pampelonne

propriétaire. récoltant. distillateur.

distillé et mis en bouteille au Chateau
MAUPAS 32240 ESTANG (GERS)

PRODUCE OF FRANCE

46% vol

70 cl

d'Armagnac, and matured in their cellars at one or the other place. No trace of 'cognarm' here, as I am glad to emphasize. Their *Chabot Blason d'Or* is highly acceptable (and much seen in duty-free outlets) their *Marquis de Monségur* is a pure Bas-Armagnac from around the Labastide area. They are advised on blending by Monsieur Loubère, a great armagnac connoisseur whose hotel (before he retired) was renowned at Labastide both for its cooking and its large range of old armagnacs.

Here, north and south of the D626, between Cazaubon and Labastide d'Armagnac and even beyond to St Justin, lie some of the finest and most secret properties. At the *Syndicat d'Initiative* in Labastide they display at least half-a-dozen of the better-known ones; but perhaps it is the secret ones you should seek out. You could motor straight through Labastide without seeing a signpost for Léon Lafitte's *Domaine de Boingnères* at Le Frèche, or the Comte de Boissesson's *Château de Lacquy*. The former is famous (throughout France, anyway) for his pure *folle blanche*, the latter for his *Reserve Exceptionnelle*, a blend of various grapes and vintages. Laffite prides himself on stacks equal to fifteen years' sales, de Boissesson on stocks equal to twenty. Compare that with what I wrote earlier about six years' being the average for the whole of Armagnac, and you will realise how much capital needs to be tied up to produce the very best; and why that best is, inevitably, expensive.

Do not expect to see much change out of £30 for either of these; at the price, I'd still say they are very much better than most XO cognacs. Nor need the sky be the limit: around Cazaubon, I have been able to locate two excellent small properties where you will find something almost as good for between £15–20. And even at the *Château de Lacquy*, if you will do without their oldest and best reserve, you can get away with under £15 for a *hors d'age*.

Turning south from Cazaubon (or north from Estang), you come across another high-quality region. Again, most large-scale maps show worthwhile *domaines* here; but perhaps I should single out that of Papolle, owned by an Englishman, Peter Hawkins. He settled there some ten years ago, on a fairly large estate (45 hectares), and has been competing nobly with the natives ever since. Whether he can do so in the long run as an absentee landlord (he has engineering interests in the north of France) remains to be seen, there was talk last year of him selling out. He has a small importer in England, and also sells at Estang in a small shop opposite the *arènes*. I would suggest, if you wish to visit his *domaine*, that you do so not from Monclar or Mauléon (where signs are easily missed), but from Estang (D32 and D225) as marked. You will then see a sign to the right showing both Papolle and the *Domaine de Maupas* (confusingly nowhere near a village of that same name, much further to the south!). The latter, about 1 km before you reach Papolle, has vintages going back to pre-war days; again, to be found on 'top tables' in France and famous even in the USA, though I have yet to see it in England.

Within the same small mapped square lie, as you will see, four other properties as part of the heart of *le Grand Bas*. The *Château de Castex* is famed world-wide and now also shipped to the UK; so is the *Château de Monbel*, but both are worth visiting all the same. *Castex*, in particular, should be seen for its magnificent courtyard almost surrounding the main building. The *Château de Maniban* does not sell direct: it is owned by the *négociants* Castarède in Lavardac, who sell this among other outlets, through the big Nicolas wine merchants' chain in Paris and elsewhere. I reckon this as one of the better bargains for taking home from the capital if you are not visiting Gascony, (see Paris section for more details).

145

Finally, in this small mapped square, the *Domaine de Saubagnère* lies, as you will note, well clear of any D road or other beaten track, or even any hamlet of that name. The twists and turns of small country lanes here need to be followed precisely on the map, or you could easily find yourself at the other end of nowhere, or merely going in circles. But *Saubagnère* is another of those fine old properties with a high reputation among connoisseurs and vintages (back to 1962) well worth sampling.

The villages to the south and east of Estang and their surrounding vineyards again offer some dozen properties not to be missed. There is Monlezun and Mormès, Laujuzan and Panjas, Bourouillan and Lias (I take them in a very rough oval circuit, as it were). Leaving Estang in a southerly direction, you will first come across the *Château de Lassalle* on your left, about half-way towards Monlezun. Here, the Baronne de Papelonne produces two brands, the more exclusive under her own name, the cheaper one as *Comte de Guyon*. The most expensive date back to 1946 – again to be seen on the tables of the best restaurants mainly. Monlezun lies, of course, at the heart of

Armagnac Laffitte, Monlezun.

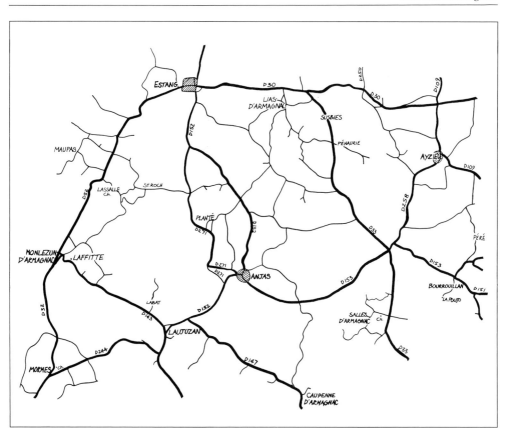

the forest of the same name, producing that dark oak best for maturing armagnacs. At the exit of the village (turning left along the D143) Monsieur Laffitte has his small property, and announces also a *dépot de champagnes* – fairly obviously to make ends meet. But double on your track to continue south along the D32 as far as Mormès, where Monsieur Spoerry at the *Château de Mormès* (left along D244) sells a fine thirteen-year-old armagnac for 160 francs. Laujuzan and Panjas hold the *chais* of *Samalens* and *Clé des Ducs* respectively; two names very well known in England, and extending a special welcome to English visitors. Also at Panjas is a *cave co-opérative* with around 250 members, producing an armagnac brand called *Duc d'Enjas*, blended from stocks up to 60 years old.

If I add very little about Pierre Cournet and his *Domaine Pléchat* (fourteen hectares) here, it is because the owner – among the most famous of the region – died recently and all was in limbo, nothing could be touched until his estate was settled. In the hope that everything has not been sold off to

Portable barrel for drinking in the fields. Wine not spirit, I trust!

one or other of the big boys, I mention merely that his treasures went right back to 1888, including most of the best vintage years also from 1914 to 1974.

At Salles d'Armagnac is the *Château de Salles*, where Monsieur Hébert ages his newly-distilled armagnacs in new Monlézun oak for five or six years. He sells a wide range from VSOP to older vintages, all unreduced and some blended from stocks going back to 1946. Be careful not to miss the turning to the right off the D153 out of Panjas; the *château* is then through the village of Salles just before you meet the D33. The church opposite it is well worth a second look, too.

To get to Boulrouillan, follow the D33 north until just after it joins the D153; this latter then almost immediately turns sharp right. There is a Michelin hotel-restaurant here which – be warned! – has a disco much favoured by young bloods for miles around. But *Le Moulin du Comte* is worth a meal, anyway and you can sample the armagnacs from at least four properties in the immediate vicinity of the village: *Larriou, Domaine de Péré, Domaine de l'Hereté* and *Le Poujo*. But perhaps you should in any case visit at least one of these, Péré to the north. Here is a property which has been run by the same family (the Dufréchous) since the time of King Louis XI (late fifteenth century), and who sell a reputable ten-years old as well as vintages back to 1928.

L'Armagnac Landais

I have already mentioned that 24 communes in the Landes *département* (as against 60 in the Gers) have the right to the *appellation* Bas-Armagnac. Of course, that reflects in part the fact that the Gers is the heartland of armagnac production, whereas both the Lot-et-Garonne and the Landes are fringe areas. But the importance of the Lande is out of all proportion to its small area – itself only a small part of that *département's* south-eastern region. It falls largely in what the locals call 'the golden triangle', the spur of land which you will note on the north western corner of the general Armagnac outline map, roughly between Gabarret and Air-sur-Adour, and bounded by Roquefort at the very north. Most of the properties nursed by Monsieur Darroze fall in this area, also important independent ones like the *Château de Lacquy* and *Château de Ravignan*. The producers of the Armagnac Landais have their own *syndicat* or growers' union. They bottle a higher proportion of their produce than any other area as *domaine*-bottled, sold at a specific age or vintage, seldom younger than ten years old, often 25, 30 or even older. The *Domaine d'Ognoas*, a showpiece which boasts its own still dating from 150 years ago, is run by and for the *département* (rather in the same manner as the *Château de Mons* at Caussens belonging to the *Chambre d'Agriculture du Gers*, at Caussens near Condom).

The pre-eminence of this small region is perhaps best highlighted by Labastide d'Armagnac and its neighbouring village of Le Frèche. Between them, they boast over twenty producers of the highest quality. Few of their names are known in England, though Gélas distributes a miniscule number of bottles of the *Domaine de Martigues* in the UK (I have seen one at Harrods at around £40 recently).

One can scour the region and still miss small properties. That of Monsieur Pierre Lauga, *Domaine de Rousseau*, lies about

5 km out of Labastide on the road to Le Frèche. He calls his produce proudly *'Bas Armagnac Fermier'*; the spirit is distilled naturally in an armagnac-type alembic and sold at various strengths according to age. Though by no means all produce or sell that very young and strong *eau-de-vie blanche* which the Gascons love to swallow by way of a *trou gascon* to clean the palate in the middle of one of their gargantuan meals.

If you are fortunate, you will find an even longer and more prestigious list of armagnacs. But you will not find these in shops, nor necessarily at the properties (indeed, some of the properties no longer exist). Monsieur Alain Dutournier, whose latest restaurant list this represents, is a Gascon born and bred, who has scoured the region for many years past. He offers his selection at *Le Trou Gascon* in Paris, at fairly mind-boggling prices. To drink your way through them all, you would need to lunch or dine there once a week for a year or so.

You can do the same, or nearly the same, rather more cheaply by visiting Lucien Legrand's emporium at 2 rue de La Banque also in Paris, not far from the Bourse *metro* station. At my last count, he had a dozen of Monsieur Laberdolive's vintages, ranging in price from £30 per bottle for a 1976 to ten

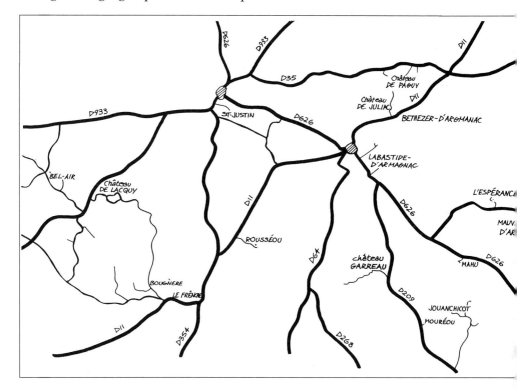

The square in Labastide d'Armagnac.

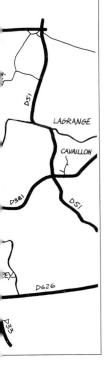

times this price for a 1935, as well as a full selection from Darroze from around 250 francs. If you wish to find more 'everyday' armagnacs in Paris, Bardou (two branches near the Gare du Nord) and the big Monoprix in the rue de Rennes, just by the Pub Saint-Germain on the Left Bank, are your best bets. I have never bought a poor armagnac from Bardou, ranging from their own selection at 75 francs to Magnol's *Domaine de La Brette* (Ténarèze), fifteen years old at 165 francs. As for Monoprix, they have occasional bargains worth hunting for: before Christmas 1988, I found here an extraordinarily pungent own brand, 21-year-old, costing just 125 francs (produced for them, as the small print on the label told me, by the *Marquis de Caussade* cellars at Eauze and classed as a *grand bas*).

There is, I fear, no such thing as a full and reliable list to producers and *négoçiants* in the region. This is not surprising, in view of the fact that around 1,400 of the 14,000 small growers are said to have a cask or two, young or old. And though you can now find 80 or so 'brands' in London, too, for reasons already given, such 'brands' are not what armagnac is all about. Go to the Landes if you possibly can, and just look around. It is not much use even looking in the business pages of the local phone directory there. If I give you just one more address here, it is because you will not find it elsewhere. It is also, almost, off the Armagnac map; and even if you look under F. de Coutard under the small village of Castandet (north east of Grenade-sur-Adour) you will find no clue to what awaits you. Which is, in fact, a splendid second Empire *château*, where successive generations of the Baron's family have quietly been producing an excellent Bas-Armagnac since 1868. I say an armagnac, because here the policy happens to be rather the opposite of many others, who tend to hedge their bets as it were. The Coutard's armagnac is always seventeen years old, and sold at a strength of 44° vol, which happens to be, according to their belief and experience both the right/ natural strength and age to show it at its best. One quality, one price (220 francs as of August 1988); and – as Monsieur de Coutard took pains to inform me – "our production being entirely artisanal, and our clients hitherto exclusively French, we have no export tariff".

So France's best-kept secret continues to be rather well kept to this day; even I have, I hope, dropped various hints rather than spoilt the market.

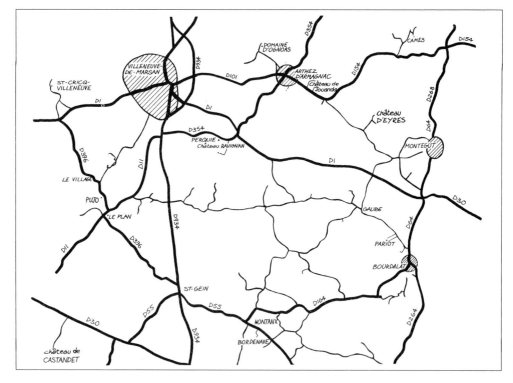

The Ténarèze

Not more than about 5% of Ténarèze armagnac production is bottled as such; the rest goes for blending. Not surprisingly, since the majority of big (comparatively speaking) *négociants* have their headquarters in this region: Janneau and Larressingle at Condom, Sempé at Aignan, to mention only three.

This makes the search for small *domaines* which bottle their own all the more exciting. They are few and far between, since it is generally admitted that a good Ténarèze needs more ageing in cask – to gain full maturity, I mean – than a Bas-Armagnac or blend. Since the process, therefore, is long and costly, not many producers can afford to indulge in it, except by way of subsidising it by way of other produce. Sempé, for example, sells its *les Cles de Saint-Pierre* (named after a vineyard of ten hectares) as a fifteen-year-old and ten-year-old, quite apart from its other brands. I have yet to see it in the UK, and I think we are unlikely to, most of it going straight to restaurateurs or luxury grocers, if not to private customers direct.

André Daguin of the famous *Hôtel de France* in Auch is a fierce supporter of Ténarèze, maintaining that any slight roughness there may be is more than compensated by depth of flavour. You may buy a twenty-year-old at the *cave* adjoining his hotel at 180 francs for the 70cl bottle (summer 1988 price). Excellent value, but he will not tell you where he bought it, of course: the bottle simply says *'pièce choisie par André Daguin'*. In other words, his personal choice from among many casks.

I made my own discoveries around Mézin, north of Condom, and at Cazeneuve. Follow the maps and make your own choice: I do not award marks in the manner of Mr Robert Parker of claret fame. I do make a comment or two concerning those which I particularly enjoyed – which does not mean to say that you will, too. In the Ténarèze even more than in the Armagnac region in general, the comparison with Scotch single malt whiskies holds good. Who is to say which is best among the Islay ones: Bowmore or Laphroaig or . . .? It depends on your taste buds.

A guide as to how and when to visit would be almost worse than useless; this varies from farm to farm. Few have an office as such for transacting business. At the *Domaine Broustet* (Monsieur Dubourdieu's property), I thought I would avoid the sacred lunch-break (12 noon to 2pm) by arriving as near as possible to 11.30. No-one around, except grandma, who showed me into what is best described as 'the parlour' of their modest farmstead. What would I like to taste? Her son-in-law would not be back from the fields until later (which turned out to be nearer 12.30). There was a ten-year-old, also fifteen and twenty years, and a *'prune d'ente'*. A spry old lady, I thought her around 65 but learnt later that she was 85. When the *patron* arrived, any idea of incommoding his lunch hour was quickly dispelled; of course he would gladly sell me a bottle or two, but would I mind if he did not use his typewriter for filling in

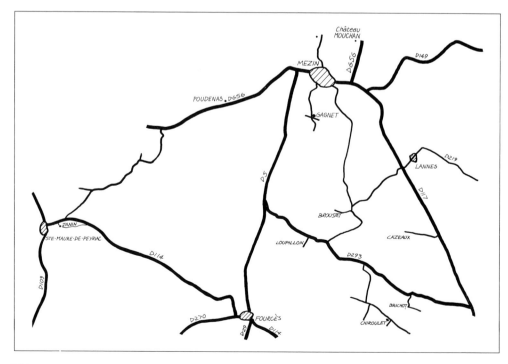

the necessary *'vignette'*. He was not very used to typing, preferred to do it by hand, slowly. So we finally parted with many *'bon voyages'* around 1pm. Nothing could have been more leisurely or more inclined to put me at my ease.

At the *Domaine La Brette* the owner was most apologetic at not being able to cope with me one mid-afternoon: he had to get a consignment off to Paris that very day and hoped I would understand about the wretched paperwork involved. Of course I did, and I hope you will, too – for these are one-man efforts largely, working often from dawn to dusk in the fields and fitting in administrative chores or customers who call on spec as best they can. Never mind: if one is too busy, there is always another one a few miles up the road.

There are, of course, exceptions: for example *Château de Cassaigne, Château de Pomes Pébèrés, Château de Pierron*: 9–12 and 2–5 or 6. Here, there are proper tasting-rooms and/or offices and no hassle about the *vignette,* because they keep tax-paid stocks ready for sale, with *vignette* impressed on the bottle capsule. Again, it is a matter of choice (or perhaps not, if you are short of time and prefer brisk efficiency to the more leisurely, lackadaisical ways of a farm). I know what I prefer – *basta*!

English is rarely spoken (you would not expect a Cumbrian farmer to speak French, would you?). And please do not

Château Pierron

CÔTES DE BUZET
VIEUX ARMAGNACS - FLOCS DE GASCOGNE
MIS EN BOUTEILLE AU CHÂTEAU
Route de MEZIN - 47600 NÉRAC - Tél. 53 65 05 52

produce credit cards or even cheques; largely unknown in this part of France and viewed with suspicion; most transactions take place in cash.

On the outskirts of Mézin, on the road (D656) to Poudenas and Sos, you will find the hotel *Les Sept Princes*, which I thoroughly recommend. Menus from 45 francs, rooms from 70 francs, everything spotless, and charming service. Like so many other inns of the region, it figures neither in *Michelin* nor in the *Logis de France* guide. Do not let this put you off, and taste their house armagnac, which comes from the *Domaine Janin* at Sainte-Maure de Peyriac, a couple of miles south of Sos. The *floc* from the same property, too, is excellent; not as sweet as some and I liked it for that very reason.

However, there are at least some half-dozen properties closer to Mézin which you should also visit, and these are shown on my large-scale map of the immediate environs. The *Domaine de Mouchan* about 2 km to the north (off the D656 to Nérac) is well signposted; they started production there only recently, so cannot sell you anything except a three-star or VSOP; but try them, anyway, at their more or less giveaway prices. To the south of Mézin, I have already mentioned Broustet and Monsieur Dubourdieu; here, there is only the most modest sign, with no indication that armagnac is produced at the farm at all. The same applies to Brichot, although this property is one of only a handful listed in the business pages of the phone directory as a producer. Both it and Cazeaux, though nominally within the boundaries of the

Château Pierron.

village of Lannes, are almost closer to Condom. Within the communes of Villeneuve-de-Mézin lies Loupillon. This is still the property of a descendant of Armand Fallières, the President of France who in 1909 signed the decree fixing the present limits of all three Armagnac regions, and who was born at Mézin. To find Claude Pinsolles at the *Château Blanc* (no more than a bungalow, this!) you had best ask at a café in the square at Mézin: it is closest of all but the most difficult to find, quite unsignposted. Yet he won a gold medal at the Paris salon of 1983 so you might like to try your luck.

This by no means exhausts the list of properties you might find within the small area bounded on the west by the D29, on the east by the D117, and by the D293 to the south cutting across country from one to the other.

I have deliberately kept here to properties lying within the Lot-et-Garonne *département*. The road which runs parallel to the D293, the D114 from Fourcès to Condom, is already within the Gers. Here, soon after it crosses the D278, you will find the *Château de Pomès Pébérès* on your left. This is one of the grander properties of the Ténarèze: Monsieur Louis Faget farms some 35 hectares and sells armagnacs at five, ten and twenty years of age. He also keeps regular business hours, which will please many. The family have owned the property for 150 years and there are old stocks going back to 1935. But the ten-year old is particularly recommended for its quality/price factor (110 francs in 1988). There is also good *floc* and – a house speciality – prunes in armagnac.

An important estate, just north of Condom.

Around Condom itself there are no less than a dozen properties within the Ténarèze *appellation*; you can get a list at the local *Syndicat d'Initiative*, just by the cathedral. A handful or so deserve special mention. There is the *Domaine d'Aula*, where they have old vintages going back to 1945. It is well signposted, to the left, along the N130 going north towards Nérac.

A little way further along the same road a right-hand turning leads across the river Baïse to the *Domaine La Brette*, already mentioned in passing. But since Monsieur Magnol's fifteen-year-old can also be found in Paris (*chez Bardou*, near the *Gare du Nord*), and he is often away or 'otherwise engaged', I suggest you continue along the same road to Plieux and Gazaupouy. Plieux is among the properties singled out in the Condom list, but it was (twice) shuttered when I called – so I cannot comment further. At Gazaupuoy, Monsieur Louis Marceilin at the *Domaine Le Couloumé* sells a very superior product, using only armagnac stills and unreduced. His family have been local squires for over 300 years; his son is currently

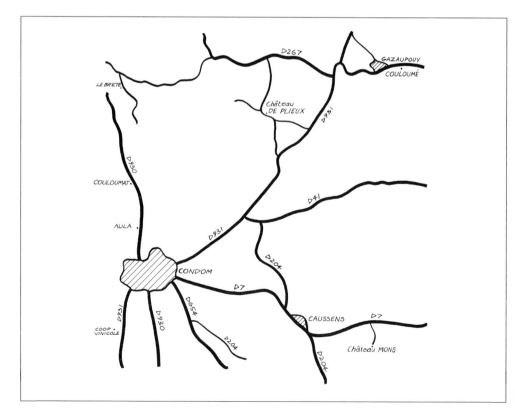

restoring the old village – well worth a look. But on no account should you miss the *Château de Mons*, a few miles to the south. This is the showpiece of the *Chambre d'Agriculture du Gers*, an experimental station as well as armagnac producer. Groups but not individuals may stay here for leisure or study purposes; long weekends are especially popular. A long avenue leads up to the *château* off the D7, a little beyond Cuassens some 6 km east of Condom. And perhaps I should have mentioned the village of Francescas, north of Gazaupouy, where at the Bar-Restaurant of the *Hôtel de la Paix* (*sous les arcades*) I tasted a 30-year-old Ténarèze officially 'no longer available'.

I may seem to have covered a great deal of ground so far, but in fact this is illusory. If you turn to your Michelin sectional map No 79, you will find all of this near the bottom of fold 14. You will see that the distance from east to west (Mézin to Francescas) is just 15 km, and from Francescas south to Caussens (on the very edge of the map) would be much the same if the route were as straight. We can say that the whole area is not more than about ten miles square. I could draw similar squares north of Mézin to Lavardac and east to Gueyyze. But I think we have seen the best of the northern Ténarèze, though I should mention *Castarède* (Pont de Bordes, Lavardac) and the *Château de Pierron* near Nérac. The former is the oldest surviving *négoçiant*, dating from 1832, just at the junction of N130 and D109, and only a couple of 100 years or

The ramparts of Gazaupouy. Louis Marcellin's family have been the squires here since the 17th century. He makes fine vintage Ténarèze armagnacs, while his son is busily restoring the old walled village.

so from the delightful little hotel *la Chaumière d'Albret* (for once, both in *Michelin* and *Logis de France* guides). The latter is just outside Nérac along the D656 towards Mézin and so well signposted as to need no map. Monsieur Hérail, its owner, is a Belgian, and produces (besides armagnac) also a *Côtes de Buzet* of good quality and value. This wine is almost monopolised by a *cave co-opérative* further north; but I am glad to see that Monsieur Herail's *domaine*-bottled one rates a mention in the 1988 special *'Vins'* issue (September) of *Gault Millau* magazine. Both it and the similarly estate-bottled armagnac are the *patron's* choice on wines/spirits list of *Chaumière d'Albret*; so you can taste them there if not at the property.

The *Château de Pierron* lies to the right of D656; cross that road (or turn to the left instead) and you are again on small country lanes seemingly leading nowhere. One of them actually does: it peters out at the tiny hamlet of Marfau. On your left, just before you get to this dead end, is the *Domaine Seugenes,* with a small board annoúncing *'la Table de Produits*

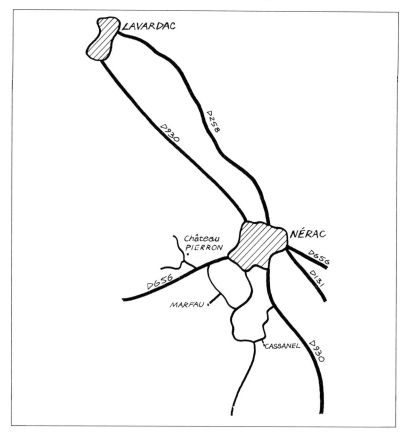

Régionaux'. There is the usual range of patés and confits and – almost by the way – a 1970 armagnac at 120 francs – well worth sampling, I would suggest. Reverse your tracks and then almost at once turn right; in another 2 km you will reach the *Domaine de Cassanel*, headquarters of an armagnac firm using the trade name San Gil. They have a list of vintages going back to 1868 at fairly astronomic prices; I can comment no further as no tastings were offered. If you turn up in a Rolls instead of a battered old Lada, you might be luckier . . .

All this can be comfortably done within two or three days, staying at Mézin as earlier suggested. I like Mézin for the huge generosity of its open square, with the large church in the centre and parking around it never any problem (what a contrast to Condom!). There is also a small museum, ostensibly open in the afternoons even out of season; but I struck unlucky. Parking spaces outside the *Hotel Les Sept Princes* are also generous – so why move, unless you have a passion for unpacking and repacking suitcases. If you stay more than three nights you will benefit by positively silly *en-pension* terms. Looking at Michelin Map 79 again (bottom of fold 13 this time) you will see that you can as easily cover the region to the east, as far as the departmental boundary where Landes, Gers and Lot-et-Garonne meet and to the south taking in Castelnau d'Auzan and Montréal. Meanwhile we have still only covered the northern fringe of the Ténarèze.

Domaine de Couloumat

BERNARD DUBOURDIEU

VITICULTEUR-ÉLEVEUR

Floc de Gascogne
Armagnac

Route de Nerac - 32100 Condom - Tél. 62 28 32 40

The canton of Montréal is the most easterly of the Ténarèze ones, with eight villages (besides the small town of Montréal-du-Gers itself) entitled to the *appellation*: Castelnau d'Auzan, Cazeneuve, Fourcès. Gondrin, Labarrère, Lagraulet, Larroque-sur-Osse and Lauraët. Take first, I would suggest, the D29 south to Montreal, a mere 13km, but with a mandatory halt at Fourcès. This picturesque circular *bastide* should on no account be missed. At Montréal, the *Restaurant Simon* is to be highly recommended for lunch. Should you try the *Château de Malliac* as a *digestif* there? Or rather the *Domaine La Boubée*? The latter has a high local reputation, the former an international one; and both are family properties still. Perhaps you should be abstemious and visit both after lunch. *La Boubée*, today run by La Veuve Ladevèze with her son, is a typically unpretentious farm, just a kilometre or so on your left out of Montréal to the east, along the D15. This property is a regular collector of gold medals, most recently in 1988 for its *hors d'age*. It is also one of the few that still cultivate older grape varieties like the Jurançon. Turn left just beyond this for the *Château de Malliac*, a real showpiece in every sense. Parts of the house date back to the fifteenth century. Since the brand *Fermiers de Malliac* is well-known here in England (distributed by Deinhard), I need say little more. Except perhaps to draw attention to a pure *folle blanche*, bottled in small quantities and only occasionally – always in 2½ litre *pots gascons*. Pricy, of course, but worth it.

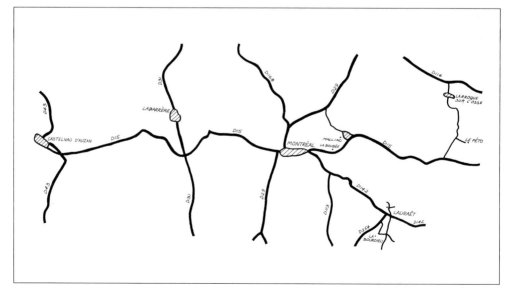

La Basse-Rivière

*T*his region of Armagnac stretches roughly from Aire-sur-Adour to Plaisance. It is also known as *'L'Armagnac Vert'* from its profusion of greenery – more forest and other farmlands here than vineyards.

Still, the vineyards are worth seeking out, the more so since on the western side of the river Adour they include one of the best wines of south-west France: Madiran. You need not travel as far south and out of your way as the village of Madiran itself, which actually lies in the Haut-Pyrenées *département*, no longer within Gers boundaries. (Unless of course, you are coming from the south anyway, from the direction of Pau, which was one of my suggested access routes.) There are excellent wines to be found of the Madiran *appellation* at Maumussan-Laguian, and also at the co-operative cellars at Saint-Mont, both of which I have mapped. Most easily accessible from Riscle – or indeed, from across the river at Termes d'Armagnac, where the *Hôtel de la Tour* makes an excellent *étape* or stop-over for the entire region. The *tour* (tower) itself dates from the fifteenth century and is now a historic monument with a small museum. To the east of Termes lies the even smaller village of Sarragachies, where Monsieur Despagnet – its mayor – was said to have produced an excellent Bas-Armagnac at a ridiculously low price until he died recently. Again (as with *Cournet* at Panjas), all was sealed and barred until the heirs had sorted out his affairs, including of course such stocks as he held.

At Luppé-Violles and Plaisance there are *Michelin*-starred restaurants; that at Plaisance has a particularly wide range of old armagnacs – at a price! Further north, towards Nogaro, lies Sorbets, where the *Château de Laubade* is one of the showplaces of the region. They own vineyards getting on for 120 hectares and make, besides a fine Bas-Armagnac an *eau-de-vie-blanc*

fairly potent and drunk at those huge gastronomic banquets, common in this part of the world, as a chaser or palate cleaner between courses (with a sorbet, incidentally). The *Château de Laubade* has devised a special range of glasses for this purpose. Apart from the standard range of miniature to *pot gascon* of two-and-a-half litres, they also do a most magnificent presentation bottle of five litres – not to be lifted, of course, but with a tap near its base.

Dartigalongue, established in 1838, is the second oldest négociant in Armagnac.

A sketch of the landscape near Nogaro.

A few miles north of Sorbets lies Nogaro, one of the bigger towns of the Bas-Armagnac and with perhaps the most important *cave co-opérative* of all. The 450 members between them grow vines over 1680 hectares; 40,000 hectolitres are distilled annually, using the Armagnac-type still only. Their price-list shows a range of nearly 50 products, from three-star to vintages; fruits in armagnac; a cocktail called *'Mousquet'* and an aperitif called *'Pinkger'*; *floc* too, of course. Their *hors d'age*

Hotel-Restaurant La Chaumière d'Albert.

blend wins gold medals at Eauze annual fair with almost monotonous regularity. I see this *Cave des Producteurs Réunis* was represented at the September 1988 London fair, which Food & Wines from France organised especially for 'lesser known regions' – and, be it added, the only armagnac producer there! I hope they found the time, expense and effort well spent, and that we may read of a UK agency soon.

Also at Nogaro is the second-oldest *négociant* in Armagnac, Dartigalongue, established in 1838. They own the *Domaine de Lacroutz* at Salles d'Armagnac and sell it as the brand *La Croix de Salles*. Only this seems to have found its way to the UK – the better and rarer vintages appear (as is so often the case) to be confined to France, or even to Gascony. Their *Trésor des familles*, for example, aged for between fifteen and twenty years, or their 1924 vintage. I hesitate to mention (yet again) an 1893, much less an 1829 which has been kept not in cask but under glass for a century or more. If you have to ask the price you cannot afford it. The establishment lies right in the centre of town, down a small cul-de-sac; any café will direct you.

Cravancèes and Loubedat, just to the east of Nogaro (with the latter slightly more to the south) are hidden among a network of small roads; and you will find even smaller properties even better hidden if you follow the large-scale map. This is one of my favourite tiny enclaves, as yet quite undiscovered by any English wine merchant I know of, yet with some half-dozen real treasures within as many half-miles. If you were to follow your nose, you might just stumble upon them – but I saw only one signpost, that to the *Domaine Lesquette*, off the D231 to the left, in the village of Loubedat. Follow the same road and you reach Sarclé, whose owner, Monsieur Henri Lamor, invented *floc* in 1974. The *folle blanche* grape flourishes here and you will find a dozen vintages from 1914 to 1963. The *Domaine de Guéchat* lies further north, off the D153 towards Manciet.

Growers are divided, just as they are on distilling of armagnacs and maturing in other than local oak. We are told (yet again) that what the public demands (except possibly in classic first-growth clarets) are wines that may be drunk young. When I first visited Gascony and stayed at Monsieur Daguin's establishment in Auch, more than fifteen years ago, this was not so: I was offered a fifteen-year-old, just about ready, and there were vintages in his cellars going back almost 100 years. It is just possible, if you show keen interest and buy a crate of more recent stuff, that Monsieur Capmartin of the *Domaine Baréjat* (Maumusson-Laguin) will fish out one of his older bottles for you to savour. His property is well-signposted (D136, on your right, before you enter the village).

Madiran

You are, in the Basse-Rivière Armagnac region, so close to Madiran, that it would be a pity not to make a day's excursion/detour. Called Madiran after a village lying south west of Castelau Rivière-Basse, this wine area is, in fact, rather larger than you might think and straddles the three *départements* (or corners of them) of Gers, Pyrenées Atlantiques and Hautes Pyrenées. You cannot go far wrong, however, if you make the small village of Aydie, some 8km due west of Castelau, your headquarters. From there it is easy to visit both Maumusson-Laguian to the north and Crouseilles to the south. At Crouseilles you will find an excellent *cave co-opérative* with a choice of various vintages; at Maumusson-Laguian both Monsieur Alain Brumont (*Domaine de Boucassé*) and Monsieur Roger Capmartin (*Domaine Barréjat*). Both have a high reputation; but their produce is so much in demand that you are unlikely to be able to buy any vintage earlier than 1986 from either of them. In London, by far the best source for Madiran wines is Sookias and Bertaut; I will say no more here, as this small firm is now famous for importing all the better wines from south west France, from Bergerac and Duras via Cahors right down to the Jurançon wines of the high Pyrenees; all are listed in the *WHICH? Wine Guide* (1989 edition). A pity they do not as yet have a spirit licence, we might be seeing many more of the better 'farmagnacs' here otherwise.

But to return to Aydie: the tiny (9 rooms only) *Hôtel-Restaurant Chez Henry* is the only place to stay, and one of those typical Gascon inns featured in no guide other than the local one by Monsieur Vidal (Ed. *Art Village*, Saint-Clar). Excellent food from around 45 francs including wine, simple but clean rooms. And at Aydie is another top producer, Monsieur Laplace at the *Château d'Aydie*. He has, or had some months ago still, a 1982 vintage.

I was told, fifteen years back, by Monsieur Daguin at the *Hôtel de France* in Auch, that you should not really drink a Madiran less than fifteen years old (he then still had bottles going back to the early 1900s). Times have changed, so have vinification methods and grape varieties (much more cabernet now mixed with the very tannic Tannat); people have not the patience to wait. But among the smaller growers of the 30-odd villages that comprise the AOC you might still pick up a bottle quite different from newer more Bordeaux-like type. It is rather like hunting for truffles, keep your nose (& ear) close to the ground . . .

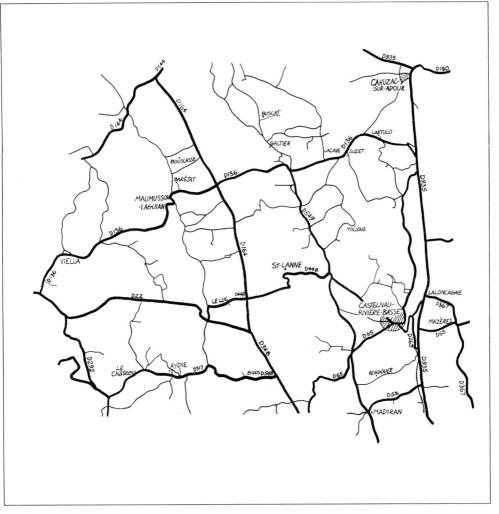

The Haut-Armagnac

*F*or the armagnac lover, this – the larger part of Gers *département* – is the most disappointing. It accounts for just over 1% of total armagnac production, with only a handful of properties bottling their own, the rest going for blending, the production of liquers, aperitifs etc. But no visitor to the region can ignore this, perhaps scenically/touristically the most rewarding part, with its capital Auch.

This last, with its magnificent cathedral, is worth at least one overnight stay. And, if you can possibly afford it, you should stay at the *Hotel de France*, owned for three generations by the Daguin family. There is little I can add to what has been written in every gastronomic guide about the culinary and other delights of this place. Adjoining it is the owner's wine and spirit boutique, where you can buy his personally selected Ténarèze, a twenty-year old quite reasonably priced (in 1988) at 180 francs. I did not see any Haut-Armagnac on sale there when I passed by last; I believe André Daguin keeps all of it, as a great rarity, for his restaurant.

What is its character? More fiery and rather rougher, they say, than that of the other two regions. Daguin admits to being something of a chauvinist in liking it; this is, after all, rugby country where rough and tough goes . . .! Not that it need be so. I would say that just as a good Ténarèze needs rather more aging than a good Bas-Armagnac, to bring out its best qualities, so does a good Haut-Armagnac – even longer perhaps, to smooth down the rough edges.

There are just two properties which matter: the *Château de Terraube*, a few miles west-south-west from Lectoure, and the *Château de Marignan* in the deep south, near Laas (north of Miélan). You will not find them any cheaper than some of the best Bas-Armagnacs; and I must leave it to you whether they are to your taste. Both properties are certainly worth visiting for their settings and architectural interest. The *Château de*

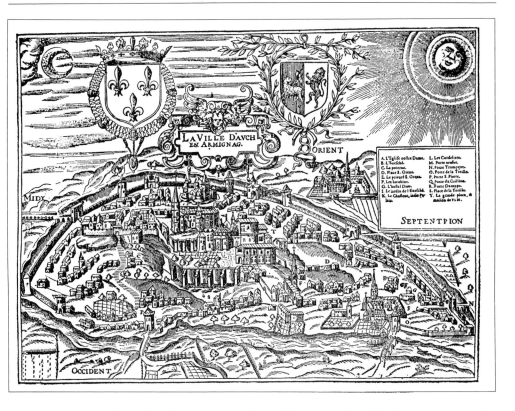

Terraube dominates the village itself, *Marignan* stands in splendid isolation and a magnificent park.

North of Auch, less than 30km up the N21, lies Fleurance, where the *Distillerie Carrère* recently (1987) celebrated its centenary. There, they use a range of old-fashioned Armagnac stills dating from around the turn of the century when these stills had reached the peak of perfection. I cannot really understand why Carrère is not represented in the UK at present. The range seems as good as that of the bigger Condom *négoçiant* houses; in addition, there is an equally good range of fruits in armagnac, an armagnac cocktail, *lou floret*, and an aperitif cocktail, *fleurette*. Vintages go back to 1942, and the *Reserve spéciale du Centenaire*, with quality lying between VSOP and Napoléon ages, seems exceptionally good value at around 75 francs (1987).

Which reminds me: should you find yourself in Toulouse, do not omit to visit Christian Lacoste at his little restaurant and delicatessen *La Mascotte* in the Place Dupuy (just by the old *Halle aux Grains*, which today serves as the municipal concert hall. He serves a remarkable 75 franc menu, and an equally remarkable range of Carrère armagnacs, as he hails from

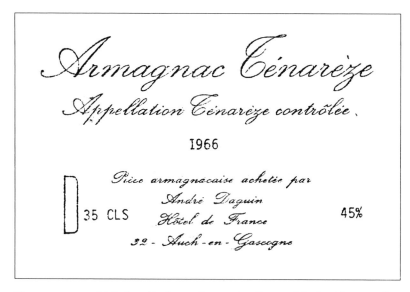

Armagnac Ténarèze

Appellation Ténarèze contrôlée.

1966

Pièce armagnacaise achetée par
André Daguin
Hôtel de France
32 - Auch - en - Gascogne

35 CLS

45%

Fleurance and his family have been dealing with that house for generations past. Like Daguin at Auch, Lacoste in Toulouse selects his own casks for bottling.

Both Fleurance and Lectoure 15km further north are worth an overnight stay if you are interested in archaeology in particular (Lectoure has a famous museum of Gallo-Romanic remains). Finally, in this region, I would recommend a visit to Bassoues. In fact this can be fitted in best with a trip to the *Château de Marignan* mentioned earlier, as it lies only about 15km north-north-west of this. Here, there is a splendid *bastide* and fortified castle-keep built by the Archbishops of Auch in the thirteenth century; while the *Hôtel-Restaurant du Donjon* is recommended for both quality and good value (menus from 45 francs, rooms from 80 francs, and armagnac by the glass from around 11 francs). And you may just get to hear (if the owners take to you!) of a third Haut-Armagnac producer close by. I am not, here, going to divulge that particular secret.

Le Guide Gascon and Art Village

*I*f Gascony is today a little more 'on the map' than it was fifteen years ago, the credit must go, to the almost single handed efforts of Monsieur Maurice Vidal. After running a successful advertising and publicity agency in Paris for over twenty years, he decided to return to his native region and founded *Art Village* – which is both the name of a small shop selling local delicacies, wines and armagnacs, and of his equally small publishing venture – some fifteen years ago.

At first, *Le Guide Gascon* was merely a duplicated sheet or two stapled together. Over the years it grew into a handsome paperback of 150 pages (1987 edition), listing 70 places to eat and/or stay at throughout Gascony, and as many wines and armagnacs of the region. For all of which, Monsieur Vidal charged precisely nothing, if you picked up the booklet at Saint-Clar or at the *Maison du Gers* (Boulevard Haussmann, Paris). And just the postage if you wished to have it mailed direct to your home address.

Sadly, Monsieur Vidal died suddenly in the Spring of 1987, just after that edition had gone to press, and when a decision to open a second outlet for *Art Village* had already been taken. His son Denis Vidal, who carries on the good work, now also at nearby Sarrant, brought out a very much slimmer edition for 1988. Still very useful, but with many addresses, particularly in the western part of the Gers and Landes, now deleted. I have not, at the moment of going to press, any news as to what may happen.

Naturally, I have drawn liberally on addresses and recommendations in the 1987 booklet, though without (I hope!) plagiarising comments. In any case, I would stress that I mention several places (e.g. *Hostellerie de Gascogne* in Lannepax) which are nowhere else featured; also, that Monsieur Vidal's *Guide* ranges much wider outside the AOC Armagnac than inside it, especially eastwards of the river

One of the grander Armagnac properties, formerly the residence of the bishops of Condom.

Gers. The village of Saint-Clar is situated east of Fleurance or Lectoure, and Sarrant is nearer Toulouse still, beyond Mauvezin (where the *Restaurant La Rapière* is specially recommended). Quite naturally, Monsieur Vidal recommends vineyards in the Lot and in the Tarn, close to him, as well as hostelries in these areas. Quite apart from the value of his *Guide*, his shop is stocked with irresistible goodies. So don't fail to visit him at 32380 Saint-Clar (Place de la Mairie, every day except Sunday).

Armagnac in the UK

Anyone who wishes to pursue this theme in depth should consult Food & Wine From France, 41 Piccadilly, London W1, who annually issue an updated list of armagnac importers. So does the annual edition of *Harper's Wine & Spirit Gazette*, besides giving trade news weekly. The most recent change I noted there was of the whisky firm, Whyte and Mackay, taking on the Camus/Chabot agencies. We may hope to see more of both *Chabot* and *Marquis de Puységur* armagnac brands in high street outlets therefore during 1989. The latter, certainly, is a Bas-Armagnac worth looking out for. Janneau is now more or less everywhere that you will find Martell; the *Armagnac de Montal*, including some vintages back to 1962, at most Peter Dominic outlets. I also saw, just before Christmas 1988, a four-year-old *Château de Lacaze* at £9.99. I would not normally recommend anything as young as this, but this may be worth an experimental tenner for the curiosity value. The property was, until recently, owned by Christopher Oldham, a wealthy English entrepreneur, who tried his hand at armagnac but rapidly (by which I mean within ten years of beginning to try) sold out to a Japanese conglomerate – whether at a large profit or to cut his losses I cannot say. Sempé's armagnacs are also putting on more of a show here now, after some shuffling around of agencies; if you were feeling flush, you could try a 1942 vintage at £62.50 (Rackhams, in Marylebone Lane). Whether the VSOP at £15+ (many outlets) is much of a bargain I rather doubt. The best high street selection by far remains that at Oddbins – a baker's (or vintner's) dozen that changes from time to time, as the Oddbins buyers find small parcels of this or that, besides popular brands such as Laressingle, Sempé, Janneau, Dupeyron and others. I wish they did miniatures, though, so that one might more easily make comparisons. Last Christmas (i.e. 1988) their 'best buy' was undoubtedly a ten-year-old *Domaine de Pléchat* (single

estate Bas-Armagnac from one of the most highly reputed villages, Panjas).

The Château de Monbel, Maupas, Estang.

Buckingham Vintners were showing an 1940 *Castarède* (more than 40 years in cask) at £62.50 good value, I thought, for one of the top (and could £225 for a 1920 at Fortnum's really be justified, by way of comparison?); Selfridges sell the very fine *Château de Lacquy* 1968 at £45 or so; while Harrods has a range that included in the autumn of 1988 the *'introuvable' Château de Briat* (unblended pure *Folle Blanche*) at £48 – 1964 vintage.

On a more mundane level, finds among smaller Bas-Armagnac properties are to be had among both smaller and bigger 'traditional' wine merchants, both in London and in the provinces. (Why no Ténarèze, when Sempé's own pride and joy is the single vineyard *Les Clés de Saint-Pierre* is a question which the Sempé agents have still to answer; probably the Armagnac region and Paris swallow most of it.)

Eldridge Pope & Co. of Dorchester sell single-estate armagnacs from the *Domaine de Théoulé* not far from Lannepax (Bas-Armagnac); although owned by Pommery Champagne, I would not class this as 'cognarm', as it is wholly made within the region. Barwell and Jones of Ipswich have recently taken on the agency for Madame Agrain's *Château Lafon*, a property

*The village of
Mauléon
d'Armagnac.*

adjacent to their more famous (& expensive) *Château Monbel.*
Also in Ipswich is the small firm of *Champagne de Villages,*
which has branched out from selling single-*domaine*
champagnes into other wines and spirits – including the
excellent armagnac produced by that other (and seemingly
more permanent) Englishman of the region, Peter Hawkins,
who owns the *Domaine de Papolle* at Mauléon, in the heart of the
Grand-Bas.

*Marcel Trépout
was firmly in
harness, aged 86,
in 1988. He is
distributed in the
UK by Georges
Barbier of Lee
High Road,
London SE12.*

Now someone has just told me of a tiny shop called *Le Gourmet Gascon*: about the size of a matchbox, in Hillgate Street, just off Notting Hill Gate. They sell all the local delicacies like *foie gras, confit* and *magret de canard,* as well as a small but choice range of armagnacs.

Licensed grocers such as Hobbs of South Sudley Street and Partridges in Sloane Street have 'exclusives' like Monsieur Guérard's *Château de Sandemaignan* otherwise only obtainable at the *château* near Barbotan-les-Thermes or at Guérard's 3-star hotel/restaurant *Les Prés d'Eugénie.*

It pays to shop around: *Les Amis du Vin* in Chiltern St W1, asks £15.75 for the *Château de Laubade hors d'age* (more than ten years old); at Berry Bros & Rudd in St James's it is £19.25.

On the other hand, Berry Bros have their own brand Fine Old Bas Armagnac at £16; while Ellis Son and Vidler sell their own (blended) VSOP at £12.50 – specially notable at this price, as it came top in a blind tasting of VSOPs – around 30 of them – held by *The Independent* early in 1988.

Inevitably, this is a selective list, and you may well find your own favourite from outside this range. And some of the very best, like Laberdolive's, are not to be found in off-licences at all, only in top restaurants such as *Le Gavroche* and *Le Manoir des Quatre Saisons.*

Armagnac in Paris

I have already referred to Monsieur Alain Dutournier's *carte des armagnacs* at his restaurant *Le Trou Gascon*, where a generous measure of 4cl can be had for anything from 30 francs to 150 francs, according to rarity and vintage. The fact that he sells only about half-a-dozen of these at his wine bar near the Etoile, *Le pain et le Vin*, and in his adjoining off-licence, *Les Toques Gormandes*, shows how scarce good old armagnacs are, and how difficult to find even for those in the know.

When you do manage to find them, they are necessarily expensive – whether in restaurants, in de-luxe grocers like Fauchon (Place de la Madeleine) or similar outlets. The top Paris wine merchant, Lucien Legrand at 2 rue de la Banque – a brief walk down from the Bourse *métro* station – is by comparison fairly reasonable. He stocks all the Darroze *domaines* he can get hold of, and also all the Laberdolive vintages. The latter range from 375 francs for a 1976 to ten times as much for a 1920.

All this is for connoisseurs. But good, even fine, armagnacs are to be found elsewhere in Paris. The Nicolas chain has its own brand, also *Château de Maniban* and *Château de Laubade* at less than 150 francs. One of my own favourite small licensed grocers or mini-supermarkets is Bardou (two branches, both near the Gare du Nord). They have an own brand at 75 francs and Monsieur Guasch's *Château de Bordeneuve* from 79 francs (this is a Bas-Armagnac, available now at different ages up to ten years old). Also the Ténarèze *Domaine de la Brette*, fifteen years old, highly recommended at under 165 francs.

I usually look in, too, at the big Monoprix just round the corner from *Le Drugstore*, in the rue de Rennes (Saint Germain-des-Près). Besides run-of-the-mill three-star brands, they sometimes have remarkable bargains by way of own brands. Just before Christmas 1988 they were offering a 21-year-old Grand Bas-Armagnac at 125 francs. The small print

told me this was produced for them by the *Marquis de Caussade* cellars at Eauze; it would doubtless sell for 200 francs upwards if bearing their label.

Then there is the *Maison du Gers*, in the Boulevard Haussmann – the official tourist promotion office that also sells a changing range of 'goodies', including armagnacs. Last time I looked in there, it was the *Château de Malliac*'s rare single-grape variety (*folle blanche*) at 450 francs. A collector's piece, since only 1,500 bottles are produced annually.

If 200 francs is your limit, you will find Sempé's 'jewel in the crown', the Ténarèze *Les Clés de Saint-Pierre* at a small grocery a few doors up from the restaurant *Le Sud-Ouest* in the rue St Honoré, just north-east up from the Louvre. No name here, but over the shopfront you will read the legend *'Spécialités du Perigord'*, including liqueurs from that region. *Le Sud-Ouest*, by the way – not to be confused with another and much more expensive restaurant in another quarter of Paris – is one of my favourite haunts for cheap, honest eating in the capital. The lunchtime menu at 52 francs includes a 25cl *picket* of house wine; their house armagnac (10 francs the measure) is De Montal. In the evening you will pay slightly more, but it would still be difficult to spend 100 francs, even including an aperitif and coffee. (Go early for lunch, it fills up quickly soon after 12 noon.)

There are, of course, many other places – too many to mention here; this is by way of a very personal short list of best buys. To explore the Paris wine and spirit scene thoroughly, you need the recently published *Paris en Bouteille* guide (Editions Flammarion – an English edition, so I am told, in preparation, but no definite news of publication here as I write this).

I have not been able to find any kind of consensus, either in the region or in Paris, as to which is the 'best' armagnac. I rather fancy there are as many opinions about this as there are armagnac connoisseurs. Monsieur Abel Sempé, in his recent book *La Grande Messe des Armagnacs*, fairly obviously likes his own 1924 vintage. But a round-robin questionnaire he sent to a number of top Paris restaurants, as well as some local ones, reveals an astonishing diversity of opinions. Some go in for vintages in a big way – notably also the de-luxe grocer Fauchon; there is general agreement that both the date of distillation and of bottling should be given. Some scour the

PREVIOUS PAGE
A turn of the century Paris café scene.

Gascon countryside for rare bottles, others deal through trade sources, be they Parisian or Gascon *négoçiants*. Fauchon's vintages go back to 1850 – no price quoted . . .! Another point of agreement is that only 'full strength' armagnacs, unreduced and bottled at barrel-proof after a number of years, are worthwhile. But opinions as to best age and strength differ widely. Dutournier of *Le Trou Gascon* prefers his at 48°–50° vol. Monsieur Azam of the *Relais de l'Armagnac* at Luppé-Violles (near Nogaro) prefers it at 42°–46° and plumps straight for the sublime 1968 from the village of Panjas, and this vintage was in January 1989 also available from Laytons Wine Merchants, Midland Road, London NW1.

The odd man out is Daguin of the *Hôtel de France* at Auch. Whereas all the others prefer the Bas-Armagnac, he is a fierce defender of the Ténarèze, where he hand-picks his own casks. According to the manner of distillation, he leaves it in cask between fifteen to twenty-five years and adds three to four years of bottle age. This is the only reference I have found to further ageing in bottles. It is generally held that there is no further change in the spirit once under glass. I am glad to find at least one expert sharing my own view that 'it ain't necessarily so'. Much, surely, must depend on the porosity of the cork used – if you use cork at all, that is, not some metal enclosure, or seal effectively against all 'breathing' with wax (a practice I abhor, if only because it makes for a messy and difficult opening of the bottle later).

BNIA MEDALLISTS 1988

COMPTE 0

BAS-ARMAGNAC
Gold Medal – GEORGACARACOS Constantin – EAUZE
Silver Medal – S.C.A. CHATEAU DE LAUBADE – SORBETS
Bronze Medal – CAVE DES PRODUCTEORS REUNIS – NOGARO

TENAREZE
Gold Medal – Vve LADEVEZE + FILS – MONTREAL-DU-GERS

COMPTE 1

ARMAGNAC
Gold Medal – SEMPE S.A. – AIGNAN
Bronze Medal – COOPERATIVE ARMAGNACAISE VITICOLE D'EAUZE

BAS-ARMAGNAC
Gold Medal – CAVE COOPERATIVE DE CAZAUBON
Silver Medal – ARRANGUA Ernest – LANNEMAIGNAN
　　　　　 – S.C.A. CHATEAU DE LAUBADE – SORBETS

TENAREZE
Silver Medal – BERAUT Gaston – MONTREAL-DU-GERS

COMPTE 4

ARMAGNAC
Gold Medal – SOCIETE DES PRODUCTS D'ARMAGNAC – EAUZE
Silver Medal – SEMPE S.A. – AIGNAN
Bronze Medal – COOPERATIVE ARMAGNACAISE VITICOLE D'EAUZE

BAS-ARMAGNAC
Gold Medal – SOCIETE CIVILE JEAN DU HAUT – PERQUIE
Bronze Medal – GRASSA + FILS – EAUZE

TENAREZE
Gold Medal – LAPORTE + FILS – CASTELNAU D'AUZAN
Silver Medal – BERAUT Gaston – MONTREAL-DU-GERS

COMPTE 5

BAS-ARMAGNAC
Gold Medal – DANDO Andre – BOURROUILLAN
Silver Medal – DARZACO Albert – BETBEZER
Bronze Medal – S.C.I. MANIBAN – MAULEON D'ARMAGNAC

TENAREZE
Gold Medal – ROUCHON Robert – BOUZON GELLENAVE
Silver Medal – LAPORTE + FILS – CASTELNAU D'AUZAN

COMPTE 10–20

BAS-ARMAGNAC
Gold Medal – CAVE COOPERATIVE DE CAZAUBON
Silver Medal – ARRANGUA Ernest – LANNEMAIGNAU
Bronze Medal – DE COUTARD Jacqueline – CASTANDET

TENAREZE
Gold Medal – Vve LADEVEZE + FILS – MONTREAL-DU-GERS
Silver Medal – BERAUT Gaston – MONTREAL-DU-GERS
Bronze Medal – ROUCHON Alix & Robert – BOULON GELLENAVE

PRIX DU PRESIDENT DE LA REPUBLIQUE

BAS ARMAGNAC – COMPTE 0
GEORGACARACOS Constantin – EAUZE

Visiting Hours of Chais

HOUSE	ADDRESS
Armagnac Vve. GOUDOULIN	Domaine de Bigor COURRENSSAN 32330-Gondrin Tel: 06-35-02
Armagnac LAFONTAN Distillerie des Côteaux de Gascogne	CASTELNAU D'AUZAN 32800-EAUZE Tel: 29-23-80
Armagnac MARQUIS DE TERRAUBE	TERRAUBE 32700-LECTOURE Tel: 06-10-03
Armagnac SAMALENS STE V.E.V.A.	LAUJUZAN 32110-NOGARO Tel: 09-14-88
BINELLI-MESTRE	29 rue Thierry Cazes 32500-FLEURANCE Tel: 06-10-10
CASTAY Frères	Château de Jaulin BRETAGNE D'ARMAGNAC 32800-EAUZE Tel: 09-90-02
CAVE COOPERATIVE DE CONDOM	Ave. des Mousquetaires 32100-CONDOM Tel: 28-12-16
CAVE Frères	LANNE PAX 32190-VIC FEZENSAC Tel: 06-36-01
CAVE DES PRODUCTEURS REUNIS	32110-NOGARO Tel: 09-01-79
LES CHAIS DES GRANDS ARMAGNACS	Route de Toulouse 32110-NOGARO Tel: 09-00-63
COOPERATIVE D'ARMAGNAC "GERLAND"	Route de Bordeaux 40190-VILLENEUVE DE MARSAN Tel: 58-21-76
CIE DES GRAND ARMAGNACS	CASTELNAU D'AUZAN 32800-EAUZE Tel: 28-42-01
DAGUIN	Rue Guynemer 32000-AUCH Tel: 05-00-45
DAMBLAT	Rue de la République CASTELNAU D'AUZAN 32800-EAUZE Tel: 29-11-11
DARTIGALONGUE & FILS	32110-NOGARO Tel: 09-03-01
DISTILLERIE CARRERE	36 rue des Alliés 32500-FLEURANCE Tel: 06-11-06
ESQUERRE-BOUNOURRE	Place des Maures 32000-AUCH Tel: 05-20-71

BRAND/MARQUE	VISITING HOURS
ve. GOUDOULIN	On application
rmagnac LA FONTAN	9 a.m.–12 noon & 2 p.m.–6 p.m. every day except Thursday & Saturday
1arquis de TERRAUBE	Saturday afternoon by appointment and all day Sunday
rmagnac SAMALENS	9 a.m.–1 p.m. & 3 p.m.–7 p.m. Monday to Saturday by appointment
	9 a.m.–12 noon & 2 p.m.–7 p.m. Every day except Wednesday and Sunday
♦. CASTAY	2 p.m.–5 p.m. Every day except Thursday and Sunday
eigneurs de Teste, Comte de Fissac, ère Max	8.30 a.m.–12 noon & 2 p.m.–6 p.m. Every weekday. Saturday & Sunday by appointment
rmagnac CAVE	4 p.m.–6 p.m. Wednesday only
AVE DES PRODUCTEURS REUNIS	9 a.m.–12 noon & 2 p.m.–6 p.m. Monday to Friday
astagnon Les Chais des Grands rmagnacs	8.30 a.m.–12 noon & 2.30 p.m.–6.30 p.m. Monday to Friday
ERLAND	By appointment only
rmagnac Etchart, Marquis de la Caze	8 a.m.–12 noon & 2 p.m.–6 p.m. Monday to Saturday. Also 2 p.m.–6 p.m., Sundays between June and September
. Daguin	Monday to Sunday, all day
AMBLAT, BARON DE CASTELNAU, ♦ESTON, LE COEUR	2 p.m.–5 p.m. Monday to Friday
ROIX DE SALLES	Monday to Sunday, all day
ANACHE D'OR	Monday to Friday, afternoons only
T CHRISTEAU, GRAND ECUYER	Every day, all day, except Thursday

Visiting Hours of Chais

HOUSE	ADDRESS
ETS GELAS & FILS	Avenue Bergès 32190-VIC PEZENSAC Tel: 06-30-11
ETS PAPELOREY	Rue des Carmes 32100-CONDOM Tel: 28-15-33
GARREAU Charles et ses enfants	Château GARREAU 40240-LABASTIDE D'ARMAGNAC Tel: (58) 44-81-08 & 44-84-03
S.A.R.L. Henri FAGET et ses enfants	Château de Cassaigne CASSAIGNE 32100-CONDOM Tel: (62) 28-04-02
JACQUES RYST S.A.R.L.	25 rue de la République 32100-CONDOM Tel: 28-08-08 & 28-13-32
JANNEAU FILS S.A.	50 Avenue d'Aquitaine 32100-CONDOM Tel: 28-24-77
MADER & FILS	Chemin de Ronde 32190-VIC FEZENSAC Tel: 06-30-44
MARQUIS DE CASSAUDE S.A.	Avenue de l'Armagnac 32800-EAUZE Tel: 09-94-22
SEMPE	32290-AIGNAN Tel: 09-24-24
PALLAS S.A.	DOMAINE DE CASSANEL 47600-NERAC Tel: (58) 65-01-51
Paul LASSERE	HON TANX 40190-VILLENEUVE DE MARSAN Tel: (58) 58-23-02
ARMAGNAC DUCASTAING	32190-VIC FEZENSAC Tel: 06-33-92
SOCIETE DES PRODUITS D'ARMAGNAC	Route de Cazaubon 32800-EAUZE Tel: 09-82-13
STE FERMIERE DU CHATEAU DE MALLIAC	Château de Malliac 32250-MONTREAL DU GERS Tel: 28-44-87
TREPOUT & FILS	Château Notre Dame 32190-VIC FEZENSAC Tel: 06-33-83
STE DELORD	LANNEPAX 32190-VIC FEZENSAC Tel: 06-36-07

BRAND/MARQUE	VISITING HOURS
RMAGNAC GELAS, DUC DE ARAVAT, MARQUIS DE ROQUE, RUNE	Monday to Friday, afternoons only
RMAGNAC LARRESSINGLE	10 a.m.–12 noon & 2 p.m.–5 p.m. Monday to Friday
s-Armagnac GARREAU	Tuesday to Thursday by appointment (Musée du Vigneron d'Armagnac 9 a.m.–12 noon & 2 p.m.–6 p.m. all year)
	9 a.m.–12 noon & 2 p.m.–7 p.m. every day
ST-DUPEYRON	9 a.m.–12 noon & 2 p.m.–6 p.m. Monday to Friday (Every day during the summer)
RAND ARMAGNAC JANNEAU	10 a.m.–12 noon & 3 p.m.–6 p.m. Monday to Saturday (Every day between July and mid September)
RMAGNAC MADER, ARMAGNAC AVARDAC	Monday to Friday, all day
ARQUIS DE CASSAUDE	10 a.m.–11 a.m. & 2 p.m.–3 p.m. Monday to Friday
EMPE	11 a.m.–12 noon & 5 p.m.–6 p.m. Monday to Saturday lunchtime between April and August
AN GIL	2 p.m.–5 p.m. Monday to Friday
OMAINE DE MIQUEOU	2 p.m.–3 p.m. Monday to Saturday
RMAGNAC DUCASTAING	2 p.m.–5 p.m. Monday to Saturday
ARQUIS DE MONTESQUIOU	On demand
RMAGNAC MALLIAC	8.30 a.m.–12 noon & 1 p.m.–5.30 p.m. Monday to Friday
RMAGNAC MARCEL TREPOUT	9 a.m.–12 noon & 2 p.m.–6 p.m. Monday to Saturday lunchtime. Saturday afternoon and Sunday by appointment
RMAGNAC DE LORD	8 a.m.–12 noon & 2 p.m.–6 p.m. Monday to Friday

STATISTICS RELATING TO ARMAGNAC
issued by
BUREAU INTERPROFESSIONEL DE L'ARMAGNAC

IN HECTOLITRES (100 LITRES) OF PURE ALCOHOL UNLESS OTHERWISE STATED	1981/82	1982/83	1983/84	1984/85	1985/86	1986/87
TOTAL SALES	43,882	36,703	31,482	35,259	32,006	32,450
TOTAL SOLD IN BULK (FOR ARMAGNAC-BASED LIQUEURS etc.)	19,432	12,309	8,276	11,678	9,669	11,314
TOTAL BOTTLED	24,050	24,394	23,206	23,581	22,337	21,136
PERCENTAGE OF TOTAL BOTTLED	54.8%	66.46%	73.71%	66.87%	69.79%	65.13%
TOTAL FRANCE	13,349	13,986	11,480	11,681	10,797	10,513
TOTAL EXPORTS	10,701	10,408	11,726	11,900	11,540	10,623
AVERAGE GROWTH OF EXPORTS	9,096	10,128	11,508	13,529	14,481	17,581
TOTAL WEST GERMANY					6,161	6,741
TOTAL JAPAN					11,862	17,142
TOTAL U.K.					10,220	18,291
TOTAL U.S.A.					25,728	28,192